This book is due for return on or before the last date shown below.

We cannot really separate individual endeavours
from social endeavours.

Oliver Sacks, *Awakenings*, p. 268

PITMAN PUBLISHING
128 Long Acre, London WC2E 9AN
Tel: +44 (0)171 447 2000
Fax: +44 (0)171 240 5771

A Division of Pearson Professional Limited

First published in Australia 1992 as *Supporting Teachers in the Workplace*
Published in Great Britain 1996

British Library Cataloguing in Publication Data
A CIP catalogue record for this book can be obtained from the British Library.

ISBN 0 273 62215 3

10 9 8 7 6 5

Printed and bound in Great Britain by 4Edge Ltd, Hockley, Essex

The Publishers' policy is to use paper manufactured from sustainable forests.

▼

Contents

Introduction

I was sitting in a coffee shop with my three-year-old daughter, idly drawing this picture on an old envelope. She too was doodling. As I touched up the crow's-feet under the eyes she leaned over, pointed, and asked, 'Is that *my* daddy?'

I admit it. I sometimes look like that in a staff room as, with my colleagues, I reach for a cuppa and mentally tune in to the next class. These days I only teach part time, but I know, I remember ... the picture describes the contours of teacher stress:

- the classroom, 8D;
- the hard student;
- the timetable loading (how did I get that class, that time-slot?);
- how I work with my peers;
- what I'm thinking about ... ;
- how I'm going to manage the 'thousand natural shocks that flesh is heir to' (*Hamlet*).

In 1988 I was awarded a travelling scholarship to the UK to research teacher stress. It was clear that teachers in the UK, as in Australia, were facing common demands, common stressors, centring on:

- the pace of bureaucratic change;
- discipline and management concerns;
- staff–staff relations;
- time and workload pressures.

While these issues were those we face also in Australia, what is clearly emerging is that the whole-school model (sometimes called the effective-schools approach) for change, plus active peer-support, is having a significant impact on teacher stress.

Research projects on teacher stress in the 1990s are legion (Otto 1986), but I've written this book more from the view of the practising teacher. How can we support one another in the workplace to cope, with some satisfaction, in a clearly onerous and demanding role? One for which, at the moment, there is little public or bureaucratic support?

It is my contention that to teach and to manage others successfully and effectively we need a supportive workplace model: no longer the isolationist teacher or the top-down model. As the OECD report *Schools and Quality* (Lowe & Istance 1989) has noted, only a clear emphasis on collegial, supportive and collaborative practices will enable schools to cope with the increasing stressors of servicing students in the 1990s and beyond. This book examines how teachers (at all levels) can bring some control to the issues directly facing them within the school environment:

- difficult students and classes;
- professional development;
- the organisational climate — the work environment;
- peer support for teachers;
- personal perceptions about stressful events;
- their own skill repertoire, especially in the area of student–teacher conflict.

There is a myth in our profession that it is the weak, ineffectual teachers who go out on stress-related illness. Not so! I've seen many 'top' teachers walk out — leave — because of poor support (sometimes none at all) from senior staff, lack of effective promotion or an unwillingness of other staff to face the need for changing practices.

Having had the opportunity of working in a large number of schools (and with a large number of teachers), I have noted a significant difference in the management of stress in those schools pursuing what is commonly called a whole-school approach to issues such as stress, management, discipline, welfare and curriculum. Differences that show up as better working relationships with pupils, more consistent work practices, clearer and more positively defined norms and goals, better working conditions and less stress-related illness. I've also noted that teachers who cope best with stress have certain attitudes, skills and approaches that enable them to cope effectively with quite significant demands.

This book outlines ways in which individuals, with their colleagues, can support one another to bring about a less stressful, more positive outlook and application to this essential profession — teaching.

I have included incidents, accounts and stories from my colleagues to illustrate the ideas and skills in this book, and I want to thank those who have shared with me their stories, their teaching experience and their correspondence. They have helped me to better understand stress in the workplace, and have convinced me that to develop effective peer support is the only way to go.

It still makes me angry that if you are 'going under', the perception is there must be something wrong with you. Also, admitting you need support usually is seen by peers and some principals as admitting that you are in some way failing, rather than simply seeing the problem 'separate' from the teacher. I remember finally admitting to one principal that I was having trouble and he asked me how my marriage was, as if to say there is something wrong with me!

That particular school had such low morale, buoyed by insensitive comments ... teachers virtually operated individually, in fear that if they opened up their reputations would be shot. For two years a general unhappiness escalated to severe stress reactions; my symptoms were so physical and alarming — insomnia, nausea, vomiting ... but the unwritten, unspoken law meant that I spoke to nobody. Weekends, holidays were no longer a time when I could recoup or revitalise or even turn off. My assessment stated I was a gifted and progressive teacher ... but for three years I lived like a pressure cooker — the fear of failure sent me to a psychiatrist, who gave me medication that dulled all my feelings so I could cope with my everyday job. This psychiatrist had spent a lot of time working with Vietnam War veterans and now specialises in teacher stress because both syndromes were similar. The troops felt as if they had no control, being in a war zone, and didn't have faith in the generals.

Joy

PART

MANAGING SELF — MANAGING OTHERS

Chapter 1

Teacher stress

Recent statistics suggest that stress-related illness accounts for up to 30 per cent of WorkCare claims. This is consistent with a number of findings (see especially *Teacher Stress in Victoria* 1989, Bernard 1990, Kyriacou 1987 and Otto 1985).

For many teachers there is a physical, psychological and spiritual wear and tear related to their job. Anyone who has to work in an environment where up to thirty children or adolescents congregate hour after hour in a room that is often small and sometimes poorly designed and inadequately furnished, and who experiences significant time and workload pressures, is bound to become 'stressed'. It's *natural*.

The causes of such stress are well-established in the literature:

- the pressure and pace of bureaucratic change (especially the demands of the changes to the Year 11 and 12 curriculum);
- the disinclination to upgrade, because of poor promotion possibilities;
- role demands: balancing teaching, administration, curriculum, discipline and pastoral roles (especially the conflict between the need to discipline and the need for pastoral care), being a 'broker' of contradictory interests;
- the plain social demands of relating to a significant number of students day after day (up to ninety a day at secondary level) not to mention parents and other staff;
- the demands of classroom management and the disciplining of 'harder' students — all the confrontational dynamics that can ensue (see chapter 3);
- administration demands;
- perception by the public — the public image;
- perception by self (personal competence, self-esteem, resources for coping;
- the school climate (how supportive or how isolationist and bureaucratic it is).

Teacher morale

Already in many Australian states, as in the UK, we are seeing an increase in teacher–student ratios. Why is it that bureaucrats think that if a teacher can teach with twenty-five students in a room, he or she can teach just as easily with thirty-five or so? ('Well, in my day ...! All you need are a few more chairs and desks.') This pathetic view — this economically rationalist view — is linked to a model of education that argues for forty desks facing the same way: teachers teach, while students listen and record, learn and regurgitate. It does not — indeed, cannot — facilitate effective mixed-ability considerations, integration, active learning or co-operative strategies.

I recently worked with a teacher who had had his Year 9 science class increased by five. So what! Five extra adolescent, large bodies. Thirty-plus students in a science classroom. No extra equipment or seats, scrounging materials, movement problems ...

What teachers want is some recognition, by those who 'administer education from the outside', of how difficult and demanding this job really is.

- The demands of teaching students of mixed ability are significant in many schools: how do you fairly and reasonably cater for several ability groups day after day?
- Certain students have significant behavioural problems of a socioemotional nature. Realistically, at a time when education is being run by economic rationalists, effective support for integration is often a 'paper reality'. Teachers struggle daily with students even visiting psychologists find hard to get through to.
- In a time of high retention — a demand placed on schools from outside — a significant number of students do not take to the academically geared thrust of the last two years

of postprimary education. Teachers are again caught between what the public demands and what social reality is. Some students are not tuned in to two years of academic study, no matter how 'good' for them it is.

I'm not saying that nothing can be done — far from it. I'm sharing briefly here the difficulty that is rarely recognised outside the schooling 'systems'.

There should be recognition of all the great things teachers do. The desire for a 'pat on the back' from the principal or senior teacher is not sycophancy, but a need for genuine recognition.

Hardly any positive reinforcement is given to many people who really feel their efforts and time given are not respected. I spend hours setting up that excursion, and not a word of 'well done' from the principal or deputy principal ...

Mary

Apart from one or two people who seem to have gone out of their way to show kindness, as a 'first year' I've felt really isolated here.

Denise

All of us, whatever our jobs, benefit from encouragement and support — from acknowledgment of our roles and their 'contribution to the whole'. Of course we can survive without affirmation, but (as any teacher knows) students and children work more effectively and feel stronger socially when they are affirmed in their progress — and we are no different. Technically, we can say that self-esteem is the esteem we ought to give regularly to ourselves; we acknowledge that our worth comes from our own positive regard for ourselves. Reality, however, confirms that we benefit — even need — social affirmation and the positive regard and understanding of others. The first social statement in the Bible (Gen. 2:18) is 'It is not good for the man [and woman] to be alone'.

How have we responded to what we know, over the past seventeen years? It is amazing that in 1991, with the technology available to us, most teachers have to wait in line in the school office to make a phone call to a parent. What other professional is left without a phone in his or her work station? At a time where personal computers are essential to almost every knowledgeable worker, teachers don't even have phones! Instead, 96 per cent of teachers spend an average of $250 per year of their own money on teaching supplies because they lack control over the teaching budget. What's more, the recent Carnegie Foundation study (1990) found more than 70 per cent of all teachers in the US are not involved deeply in decisions about curriculum, staff development, grouping of students, promotion and retention policies or school budgets.

Carl Glickman, 'Pretending not to know what we know'

Discipline problems

Many teachers are not trained to cope with the kind — and degree — of disruptive behaviour they are experiencing today, especially at secondary level. In all the stress surveys I have read or conducted, a high 60 or 70 per cent of responses feature anti-social or disruptive behaviour:
- resistance to teacher direction;
- argumentativeness or procrastination;
- defiance, even swearing at the teacher — certainly insolence, perceived by the teacher as a disregard of the teacher's role;
- frequent 'lower level' — but still frustrating — behaviours such as calling out and talking out of turn (noted in the 1989 Elton Report as a significant disruption).

There are effective, whole-school approaches to all these problems provided that schools work on a collegiate model in addressing them.

> Why should I put up with all this crap? ... I was trained to teach students, not to argue and fight with them. What really —— me off is that one day they can be almost reasonable and the next day 'off the planet'. I shouldn't have to put up with that — I mean, I can't solve their home problems, can I?
>
> *Michael*

Teacher self-esteem

It is clear that people with high self-esteem feel better, work better and deal with stress more effectively than those with low self-esteem. The former are confident about themselves and their contribution to their work, to the development of their students, to the team. In Coopersmith's terms (1967), they have a positive sense of 'identity', 'security' and 'belonging'.

It is also clear that the way we treat others reflects how well — how affirmatively — we value ourselves (apart from others' esteem). If we are insecure and uncertain of our abilities, if we feel worthless, feel an acute sense of failure, feel anger that we're 'not noticed enough', that 'others are talking about me', that 'no one understands me', it will have an effect on our students and our colleagues. It's quite dispiriting to sit in a staff room where a significant number of teachers like this coalesce!

If teachers are going to give some strength to their self-concepts (their pictures of themselves, with all their strengths and weaknesses), then they will need to learn to balance the messages that:

- they give to themselves (see pp. 16–17);
- they give to others (how critical, supportive and encouraging they are to students and colleagues);
- they receive from others (how they internalise and cope with critical, carping, cynical and whinging colleagues, let alone students).

Our self-esteem (our sense of our own value) and our self-concepts can be changed. While it is true that others can strengthen the way we value ourselves and our abilities — and there is a lot that senior staff, especially, can do in this area — we too have (and can strengthen) the ability to paint new and different, stronger, healthier, more balanced concepts of ourselves.

Remember — self-esteem *is* just that — *self*-esteem: valuing yourself as a person, accepting yourself with your strengths and weaknesses but seeking honestly to address them instead of blaming others, the 'system' or the 'present situation'.

The way we think about ourselves affects how we feel and, consequently, how we behave in our jobs, how we relate to others, how motivated we are, how confidently we can address our role as teachers.

For example, how do we label events that are stressful? How do we deal with a lack of acknowledgment from senior staff of the effort we expend? How do we deal with a lack of backup or support?

While it is legitimate to state our needs with appropriate assertion, we will feel worse and have less esteem for ourselves if we rely and *depend* on others to create our worth as a person. Children generally need the appropriate esteem of others to be able to develop a healthy self-concept as adults, though we need to balance self-approval and affirmation with the bonuses of other esteem.

That fact notwithstanding, it's pleasant and thoroughly nice (and rewarding) to actively affirm other people. It's a two-way street. All I'm saying is this: don't bank on affirmation from others, or complain bitterly if it's not forthcoming.

It is nice, enjoyable — wonderful even — to receive esteem from others: the acknowledgment of a job well done, the backup, the encouragement, but it will not always be there. One of the indicators of a healthy level of self-esteem is the ability to separate, in terms of our self-worth, what happens to us from what we eventually are.

W. A. Rogers.

If I spend a lot of my psychological energy, my thinking and emoting, on demanding approval from others — determining my worth by what others say, I'm going to feel worse (much worse) when it doesn't come. You may be in one of those schools where the senior staff do not make any significant effort to value *you* and your contributions. Assuming you're not a lazy, indifferent, uncaring teacher who may make it easy for others to 'reject' you, you can learn to *accept yourself* as you are — with an honest appraisal of your faults.

This doesn't mean, as Michael Bernard (1990) has pointed out, that you *simply* accept yourself as you are, but that you try to change for the better what is bad, ineffective and damaging to your health and wellbeing.

It is the difference between dependent recipients and active participants.

6

The role of senior staff

Senior staff need to recognise the human benefit (not merely the utilitarian benefit) of esteeming (valuing) others.

- Show an authentic interest in teachers' work. Ask pertinent questions about what they are doing.
- Focus on the strengths displayed by staff.
- Recognise and acknowledge effort; show pride in the achievement of the staff.
- Model respect even for those you dislike. Respect is shown in an action — even the pedestrian smile, the use of a first name, the words 'good morning' or 'hello' will convey it.

    I've worked with senior staff who actually walk past colleagues (let alone students) as if they don't exist, giving not even a cursory acknowledgment of their presence!
- Be available to give support when asked, and look for ways to offer it, where appropriate, without causing unnecessary embarrassment — not with a staff-room invitation to a struggling teacher: 'Oh, Tom, I believe you're having a few problems with the Year 10's? Do drop in to my office today and let's see if we can't help, eh?'.
- Set up opportunities for peer-support groupings to act as a problem-solving and professional-development focus across the school (see chapter 7).

Most of the ways in which we can esteem others are 'small beer' when set down on paper, but they have a significant effect in the long haul.

Distress

It is relatively easy to put together a few phrases to define stress. Distinguishing it from other concepts is another matter. For example, although stress and burnout are regarded as different, this distinction is difficult to observe empirically. Similarly, the difference between teacher dissatisfaction and teacher stress is not clear.

Teacher Stress in Victoria

We all encounter similar demands on our energy, time, skill and experience, but naturally we do not all respond in the same way. We all feel stressed from time to time in our jobs; the problem comes when we have great difficulty in *balancing* whatever resources we have with our ability to cope when the stressors begin to chip away at those resources (our personal, social and emotional/psychological resources, our skills, our level of health). It is the *negative* stress —and the amount of it — that is the problem, and this involves not merely the demands themselves but how we perceive and respond to those demands in the long haul, both as individuals and as a team.

Where the distressing feelings seem to take over and the feeling (and obviously the belief) of not being in control occurs is where we feel what we commonly call 'stress'. Where we manage this occupational hazard, we cope; where it is not temporarily alleviated, it can lead to a 'burnout' syndrome.

When the weekends do not effect their normal repair and rebuilding of functions, when relationships at work or at home — or both — are significantly strained, when you are still feeling fatigued, jumpy and overreactive even on Monday, it's worth taking a break to reassess — to discover whether you are:

- lacking energy, regularly tired or lethargic (that's me!);
- having sleep and appetite problems (me, too!);
- finding difficulty in making decisions (not again?);
- overreacting to situations that others *seem* to be managing well;
- feeling increasing self-doubt and lack of motivation.

All this can happen to very effective, proficient and good teachers.

Burnout is not always easily or readily apparent. It is characterised by high expectation, impatience, growing frustration, a fatigue that affects body and soul. Ultimately it may lead even to a kind of 'spiritual' numbness and detachment, a cold cynicism.

In the September 1981 issue of *Time Magazine* there was an essay entitled 'The Burnout of Almost Everyone'. It had an illustration of a crumpled 'businessman' with no head — just a burnt-out wick with smoke wafting upwards. The hands were outstretched, pleading. The essay is symptomatic of an age that expects much — demands much — from society, from interpersonal relationships and from that universe called self.

'Most of the world's work', it says, 'is done by people who do not feel well'.

In working with schools on developing a whole-school focus, it is often not surprising, initially, to find teachers working as social and professional isolates — in some cases having no idea of the needs of others or of the successful strategies others might be using.

However, if peer support is going to work at any level it needs to be elective — offered, planned and supported by the leadership team.

How teachers feel when stressed

Russell et al. (1987) have noted that researchers have consistently found that individuals who possess high levels of social support are in better physical and mental health than those who do not. Teachers classified as 'burnt-out' spent less time with their fellow workers than did other teachers. In one study (Schwab et al. 1984), a random sample of school teachers in New Hampshire found that higher levels of social support from colleagues were associated with lower levels of burnout. This is confirmed by Australian research on peer support (see Bernard 1990).

Having worked with many teachers who either had had multiple days off for 'stress-related illnesses' or who had been on WorkCare claims for stress, I have observed a mix of anger and powerlessness in their feelings about the situation.

Anger is felt towards a bureaucracy they felt had let them down or a principal who had not 'understood', or even towards themselves at 'having failed' in teaching. There is something about teaching that makes those for whom it doesn't work out as a profession feel a greater sense of acute failure and 'self-downing' than people in other professions (say, bank clerks) experience in similar situations. Blame of 'self' or 'others' is a typical reaction, because one may see oneself as the victim of others' machinations. Often the acutely stressed teacher perceives that 'others' have 'planned this', 'done that' or 'are saying this about me' and consequently *an objective assessment of the individual's condition and future is difficult.*

Powerlessness is just as self-defeating. Low self-esteem is related to damaging beliefs about oneself or one's role. 'I'll never make a good teacher.' 'No one understands me.' 'I always fail.' This passive role — almost that of a victim — is exacerbated by these self-defeating beliefs.

When help is offered, such teachers increase this self-immolation by saying: 'I tried that and it didn't work' or 'That would never work for me', 'I'm different — it's just not in my personality to do that'. In the Melbourne University (1989) study *Teacher Stress in Victoria*, it was noted that teachers on WorkCare offered 'self-defeating' patterns of explanations that showed a tendency towards blaming external factors when things did not go well. They also tended to engage in self-blame (p.30).

There are certainly unthinking, immature and unreasonable senior staff members, colleagues and bureaucrats, but of course it is never as simple as 'it's all *their* fault' ('they' being the Ministry of Education, the school, the principal or the students) or 'it's all *my* fault'. Blame of self or others, while 'natural' (even convenient), works against change of self or change of systems.

This will be explored *in balance* with the need for principals and senior staff to develop school-wide approaches to deal with stress on a preventative level.

Community misunderstanding

How many times do we hear unmitigated nonsense from acquaintances — even from friends and family — about our profession. 'Oh, you only teach 9.00 to 4.00 (if that!).' 'You get all those holidays each term!' 'Your classes are *so* much smaller these days.' 'You're always striking.' 'Why has my son had four teachers already this term?' 'Discipline?! In my day the teacher knew what to do ... we're too soft on them. They need a good —— !'

Everyone is an expert on education; everyone knows what's wrong and what should be done. And the media hype rarely addresses the positive, effective areas of education. The more common headlines are such as 'Crisis in our classrooms' or 'Twenty per cent of seven-year-olds can't read or spell or use the four operations'. Rarely is the public told about the majority of teachers who plan thoroughly, who day after day put up with sometimes emotionally traumatised, learning-disabled students.

We have a multiple role as teacher, social worker, counsellor, confidante, values clarifier, and we have to pick up the tag that some parents blatantly leave behind. This can (and often does) have an effect on our corporate self-esteem as teachers. You can sometimes see it in the jaded and dispirited faces in the staff room. When a profession is repeatedly harassed, when resources are increasingly being taken away at a time when we have more students from emotionally unstable home settings, when we have to cope with an increasing number of behavioural disorders (again without the promised support), teachers wonder: 'How important, how significant, is my profession?'. It is in fact a significant profession.

Just a teacher?

I used to say 'I'm just a teacher' when I was asked at a party: 'What do you do?' Worse, I hear colleagues saying: 'I'm just a primary teacher'. The ease with which some teachers, in a sense, put themselves down is quite telling.

Some time ago a colleague of mine made the point to me that we ought to respond to this question with: 'I'm a professional educator — I teach. What do you do?'. To the reply, 'Oh, I'm a barrister (or a solicitor, or an accountant)', we can then remark: 'Well, you must have had a good teacher!'.

Education, even within the 'formal' structure of western schooling, is a critical factor in a young person's development. We hear governments rave on about economic restructuring, yet the beginning of a healthy workforce is an educated workforce in which there are young people who are not merely employable, but who have the skills to express themselves, who can think for themselves, who have a strong sense of self-esteem and who have learned to solve problems, not just to create them. We need to support one another in a professional way and to endorse our many fine contributions to the educational experience of young people.

We can do this by acknowledging ill-informed preconceptions for what they are, and where possible:

- inviting parents in to our schools to see and participate in learning experiences and in discussions about more effective ways to discipline and manage children;
- working collegially rather than in isolation;
- publishing our success;
- improving the quality, the look and the functionality of our workplace.

Research by Russell et al. (1987) and Kyriacou (1981, 1986) has shown that supportive social relationships can help to cope with and reduce stress, especially when teachers feel they can call on others to support them without imputation of failure. The welfare (wellbeing) and support of staff — all staff — is essential to the effective running of a school. Social support will not eliminate stress, but it will provide the resources to manage it; to paraphrase Stephen Glenn, social support provides a network of fellow travellers. Such support, commonly called peer support (Rogers 1990; Bernard 1990, 1991), can:

- lessen or remove the feelings of isolation;
- provide structural, moral and professional support;
- provide a forum for problem solving, problem analysis and action planning;
- give essential stress-relieving support in the management of particularly difficult and disruptive students.

A report by Hedley Beare (Professor of Education at Melbourne University), *Skilling the Australian Community*, noted that the morale of educators in general is sagging as they face almost impossible demands and uninformed criticism from the public.

The business sector of the community [is] dominating the debate and making the most 'insistent and extensive prescriptions' about schooling. Noting that a concern with Australia's economic performance was natural, the report asked whether it was not possible to think of things more ennobling than making money.

Education Australia, 1988, Issue 2, p.12

What stress does to us

Feelings, emotions
Most often in stressful situations we think of feeling stressed, being stressed; we feel negative frustration, anger, anxiety, fear, tension, hopelessness, a 'down' feeling — we may even feel guilty for having such feelings! But these emotions are the body's warning signals that some pressure, some demand on our need to cope is there.

Behaviour
We might go on the attack: 'I'm sick of your stupid behaviour, Jason! (or 8D)'; we might act lethargically, be withdrawn and isolate ourselves because we feel depressed or believe no one cares. We might lose (or find) our tempers, or internalise our anger for fear of 'exploding'. There are many ways to act stressfully.

Thoughts, beliefs, perceptions
Is it a threat? Is it familiar? Can I cope? What if I fail? What's going to happen? I can't stand it! Blast! Damn!

The way we think — especially our *characteristic* way of thinking — will affect our level of negative stress and our ability to cope.

Body responses
All the bits and pieces inside start helping us (the general-adaption syndrome). Blood pumps around and the heart rate goes up, as does the breathing rate; muscles tense up, adrenals start pumping as though the body has to *do* something. Something out there (or inside) is stressing us, putting pressure on us to act. So responding to stressful situations is what this book is about: getting some balance, some equilibrium, into our lives as teachers.

Check it out
Prolonged, unmanaged stress can result in psychological and physical discomfort, even sickness.

It can affect family relationships and home as well as work and relationships at school.

It can cause irritability, restlessness, the tendency to become easily annoyed and the feeling of not being able to do any one thing well, and this can lead to depression and illness. Whether it is the regular feeling of tiredness and being drained or the more frightening anxiety related to pains in the chest, stomach or bowel, it is wise to consult a doctor. Those palpitations or dizzy spells, shallow breathing or 'different' pains may have no physical cause, may be anxiety-driven or anger-related hypertension, but it's worth the comfort of a medical opinion or even tests. Take a week off to get sorted out and get advice.

I've worked with many teachers who really believed that those 'pains' meant a heart attack or a tumour (as they well could), and a week or two of leave to check it all out, regroup and get medical or even psychological assistance helped enormously. Of course, it may take longer than a week or two. Seek the collegiate support and counsel of a trusted senior colleague and then explain the problem, in privacy, to the principal. With some principals this collegial support can act as a clearing house and advocate, if necessary. Setting priorities like this gives you the sense of taking charge, but support is essential. Let someone know about the problem early, and plan to get advice, counsel and help. It's your life, your wellbeing, and it's important to take time out before it takes you out. There is no stigma attached to such a course unless you believe it to be so. This is your career, your life — and our lives are more (much more) important than our jobs.

There are many excellent texts in this area and they are summarised in Bernard (1990).

Senior teachers can help, if they see signs of recurrent stressful behaviour in their colleagues, by supportively inviting them to sit and talk things through. They can suggest a week off to review, to check things out, to reassess.

Exercise and health

Teaching is an energy-depleting job. Along with a balanced diet (most of the time), some form of regular exercise can help. Even a brisk walk three or four times a week can help. In *Psychology Today* (March 1989) George Chrousas of the National Institute of Health, USA, points out that arousal and wellbeing are the outcomes of relatively vigorous exercise (say vigorous walking, jogging or swimming). Exercise scientist Daniel Landers (ibid.) outlines research that shows that people are often in a better mood and even think faster during or after exercise.

- 'If you perceive you've got more energy, you'll approach tasks you might not otherwise try.'

Check with a doctor, experiment, and slowly build up a level of exercise that can (along with reasonable diet) keep the machine well serviced!

▼ Chapter 2

Perception and stress

The most interesting trait linked to stress appears to be that which characterises differences between those individuals who believe that things in their lives are generally within their control (a belief in 'internal control') and those who tend to believe such things are generally outside their control — attributable primarily to luck, fate, powerful others, or essentially unpredictable (a belief in external control).

Chris Kyriacou, *Effective Teaching in Schools*, p. 194

Teachers — indeed, people generally — respond to stress in different ways, as Kyriacou and others have pointed out. Notwithstanding all the many facets of schools and teaching that can elicit stressful emotion, our perceptions can affect how stressful a situation is, how stressful it continues to be and how much the stress interferes with health and professional outcomes.

Take the older teacher who is really struggling with some difficult classes. One may say: 'Look, I must be able to manage those students. After all, I've been teaching for fifteen years; I should be able to deal with them by now ... dammit! they should respect me, I'm nearly forty!! I'm their teacher'.

These self-demands, expressed as characteristic beliefs that then interpret reality as inherently 'malign', will increase what is already a stressful situation. If the teacher then compares a younger teacher's ability to manage the class more successfully, and says: 'I should be able to do as well, or better', 'It's not fair (it — the world — should be fair to me!)' or 'I can't stand those kids, this situation ...', then these sorts of beliefs and the self-talk that compounds them will contribute significantly to the stressful emotions of frustration, anger, anxiety and 'feeling-down'.

Of course, stressful events *contribute* to our stress: the rude student, the uncaring principal, the unfair or poorly organised timetable, the poor working conditions and our state of health will surely contribute, but we still perceive and say things to ourselves *about* those events, and in this we have some control of the degree of stressful emotion we experience.

Research in this area has shown, in study after study, that the way we perceive and process events, and what we say to ourselves about those events, has a direct impact on how stressfully we feel and manage them. We all, from time to time, say: 'I should do so and so' or 'They shouldn't do so and so'. Where this is a relative demand, well and good ('I should get the lawn cut'), but where it is an *underlying characteristic* demand it creates a stressful condition. It is the true idée fixe, where we make an absolutistic demand on reality. 'Children *must* respect their teachers!' If this belief is running rapidly through the head while Jason and Dean are calling out, and if the equally stressful belief, 'I must have total control of the students', is also present, not only will my behaviour be more reactive, I'll feel more stressed.

If Paul, when I direct him to go back to his seat, answers back: 'What yer picking on me for?' (complete with pout, sulk and latent hostility), I'll feel threatened, I'll feel personally attacked because of my belief in high status and 'respect', and I'll probably overreact. 'Don't argue with me! *I* told you to get back to your seat now, I'm sick of your stupid complaining — you never do as you're told!'

'But they shouldn't answer back and be rude! They shouldn't swear!' Well, maybe they shouldn't:

- in an ideal world;
- if they had better social skills, better conditions at home;
- if they didn't use attention-seeking games in order to gain a sense of purpose in the group.

But just saying 'He *should* obey me', 'They *must* respect me' or 'I can't stand it when they muck around!' flies in the face of social reality. I could make demands like this on myself (and others) all day and it wouldn't change reality. What it would do is create, along with the already stressful situation, more stress.

The not-so-hidden agendas of status, demanded respect and threat to authority create dysfunctional outcomes; where reality (the arguing, pouting student) presents a severe mismatch with the demanding belief, not only do we feel worse (more angry than we need to be), our actions are more dysfunctional. When this happens regularly, the contribution of such thinking is itself a significant stressor.

This is not to deny the social wrongness of student behaviour — we need to address that; but it does mean that inflexible thinking, such as 'I must be approved of by my students or I'm not a worthwhile person', 'I must never get angry with students', 'others must be fair or I can't stand it' or 'children must respect their teachers and it's awful, terrible, when they don't' leaves little or no room for effective management of self or of others. Just regularly telling oneself that things 'must be ...' or 'should be ...' doesn't guarantee (or even make it possible) that reality will accommodate itself to those demands.

'I'll never be able to manage the class' is itself an overgeneralisation of the reality — a reality that is *very* difficult (given the social mix in, for example, 8D). But to add to this overgeneralisation beliefs such as 'I can't stand it' will make it extremely difficult to tolerate attention-seeking behaviour, or frustration generally. The belief overrides the capacity, when under pressure, to relabel an event as 'annoying, but ...' or 'uncomfortable, but ...'. The 'but ...' will need to include a plan that says: 'OK, I know this situation could be stressful, so I'll plan some strategies — what to say, what to do — and, if the student refuses reasonable directions, redirections or clear 'choices' and consequences — how to direct him (or her) from the class so that I can follow up later'.

I was working with a high-demand teacher a few years ago. She had said she couldn't stand kids who called out in class: 'They should respect me and the others' (even though Damien clearly wasn't respecting others at the time). She tended to regularly tell him not to call out, adding 'I won't tell you again!', and then in frustration send him from the class.

We had agreed to do some peer-coaching, and I was teaching in her room one day while she was observing. I was modelling *tactical* ignoring of behaviour (as one of several short-term strategies for management). Damien leaned back provocatively and called out: 'Eh, Mr Rogers, I need your help!'. I could see him out of the corner of my eye, but chose to tactically ignore him while working with the on-task students. I hasten to add here that I would only use this approach in certain circumstances:

- for calling out or low-level attention seeking (for instance, with some tantrum behaviours);
- if there were only one or two students doing it; and
- if (as in this case) it was not significantly affecting the rights of other students (this is referred to later in the section on classroom management).

Well, Damien called out again; then there was a pause, and again a slightly longer pause. The next time he called out he added the 'fit-of-pique', complete with eyes raised to the ceiling and sighing — in effect, saying 'C'mon, you're not noticing me!'. Six or so 'callings-out' later, the observing teacher strode across the room to Damien and said: 'Can't you see Mr Rogers is not taking any notice of you! What's wrong with you?'. She was tense, and said it with high emotion, handing him on a platter just what he was after — overservicing. Clearly she couldn't stand it, and (re)acted as a result of that belief.

If I regularly and *characteristically* say 'I can't stand it when they call out' (or whatever), I'll feel different from the way I will feel if I say just as regularly: 'OK, it's annoying when they do that, but it's not the end of the world. So what's my plan? What will I say and do when ...?'.

'I don't like it, but ...' is also an accurate description of reality. It's replacing one *thinking habit* with another.

> Man is the only animal on earth rationally capable of describing his thoughts as rational. All the rest of the animal kingdom think we're bonkers — particularly the dolphins and the chimpanzees, who've been bored out of their minds with decades of mazes and electrical shocks and think that B.F. Skinner is a passé old pervert.
>
> Dr Robert Buckman (1987)

Control

The degree to which we feel — and, as importantly, *believe* — that we have some control over stressful situations determines how effectively we manage stress. If we've chosen teaching, we've chosen a stressful profession — there's no question about that. There are many situations in life and in our profession that we have no direct control over; we have perhaps some negotiated control but little direct control. It is at these times (concern at one extreme about being stuck in a traffic jam and at the other about being landed with a 'tough' class) that we need to realise that if we cannot directly control or govern events that are stressful, then we need to govern ourselves and to control:

- our thinking — the way we characteristically perceive, think about and speak to ourselves about stressful events;
- our reactions and our responses — how we characteristically respond or react (Do we know? Does it help? Can we change our responses? To what? How?);
- the skills that may minimise the stressful effect;
- the way we organise time, a lesson, our room, ourselves, our health.

We cannot escape stress, but if we can bring some control to these areas we can learn to live with it. In some cases it can even energise and call forth the best in us.

Thinking habits

Habits change into characters.
Ovid (45 BC–AD 17)

We all use internal dialogue. Sometimes it's quite active and conscious; sometimes we're barely aware of its impact on events. Cognitive psychologists contend that inner speech — self-talk — has 'a powerful impact on emotional wellbeing and motivation' (Braiker 1989).

Self-talk, like any talk, will serve us better if it's realistic and truthful; there's not much point in bulldust in our own heads!

Psychological junk mail

Peter has had a particularly difficult class, and after the class says to himself: 'I feel an absolute failure. I know I should be better prepared. I know I shouldn't scream at them, but I've given up trying to be reasonable. Damn it! Its just not fair. Why should I get the rotten Year 8s? I always get the raw end of the stick. I'll never manage them'.

Here are plenty of loaded statements: 'absolute failure', 'shouldn't scream' and the faulty assumptions of 'it's not fair', 'I've given up', 'I always get ...', 'I'll never ...'. These distortions and generalisations, if they are a regular feature of one's self-talk, need correction. If the assumptions behind them are overtly demanding ('life must be fair, I should never get angry' instead of 'life *is* unfair, difficult, hard, not easy'), it will be all the more difficult to cope. Reality will confirm our darkest suspicions.

'I shouldn't get angry.' Why ever not? I've had many classes where I've been angry (feeling mild to high anger). The real issue is not whether we should or shouldn't be angry; feelings, emotions in themselves are not bad or good — it's what we do with them that counts, how we can communicate why we're angry and what about.

When we rephrase our self-talk, we are remapping reality — refocusing. Of course we need skills, social support and organisational support for a healthy workplace, but if we do nothing about our working beliefs, our self-talk, the job is only half done. In fact, we may not always be able to change external events and situations directly. We can, however, do something about the way in which we perceive these events and speak to ourselves about them.

'OK, I know I'm having some trouble, especially with those three boys (be specific). I may have failed in some things, but no one is perfect — it doesn't make me a failure. It's natural I'll get angry, but if I work on my management plan I'll become less reactive and I can learn to *use* the emotion of anger. So! 8D isn't a fair timetable slot, but others have them, too. I'll just have to do the best I can with them. Michael has them and he seems to be coping reasonably well; I'll discuss it with him. I often muck up, but I've had a few good sessions; now, what made these sessions work?'

This is not mere badinage. Talking, even self-talking, is an action, and actions have effects. If I say 'I'm no good', that is overgeneralising. If I have a demand behind it ('I *must* get it right all the time'), I'll set an impossible pace. If, however, I say 'Look, I'm having difficulty with ...' and 'What skills and support do I need?', that is *accurate* self-talk. Being more accurate and reasonable will help me in addressing my goals.

Inaccurate, inflexible, demanding and negative self-talk may become a habit. If not addressed, it may become so characteristic that it is no longer a conscious activity. And while past performance and past experience may have interred our characteristic self-talk, it is in the present that we are using it and in the present that changes need to be made.

> In one of my classes, I'd arrived late. I could have kicked myself. The class was already hyped up — they normally are after music — *then* I'd forgotten the hand-out stuff! I tried to apologise, and the class sighed as if I'd meant to forget. To top it off, the VP came in; he could see I was hassled, but all he was interested in was the report I hadn't finished.
>
> *Bruce*

To this experience, this teacher then adds self-talk of the order of 'I'm an idiot — I really wrecked that. They'll think I'm stupid. It's awful. Why did I do it?! I really screwed up!' If he says this over and over (not merely en passant), he actually takes the actual failure (he did 'fail') and turns it into self-judgment. This is what Edwards (1977) calls 'mentally kicking oneself'.

If we add to the mistake or failure a litany of self-statements as above ('I should have! I'm stupid ... an idiot!'), we only strengthen the feeling of failure. This has a twofold outcome.

- We feel worse than we need to feel. Naturally we will feel 'bad', let down, put out; we don't need to compound it with psychological junkmail.
- We'll find it harder to cope with the failure and/or improve in the area where we're presently 'failing'.

Excusing

We could also say, as a kind of mental brush-off, that it doesn't matter — when clearly it does matter. This failure *is* annoying; it has an effect. It doesn't help to deny the natural feeling of failure, to say 'It'll just go away'. It won't. 'It doesn't matter what I do.' It does. Self-talk is a response to events and our feelings about them. Realistic self-talk can help reshape reality and enable us authentically to start again.

Tuning in and rebuilding

As Harriet Braiker (1989, p.26) notes:

> How you respond to your self-talk makes all the difference. ... for the negative thoughts you've uncovered, just identify how they are wrong, then argue actively with yourself to correct the errors.

- When what happens in your life doesn't fit with what you'd expected or predicted, unhelpful self-talk may be the cause. ('It shouldn't have happened!' 'It's just not fair!')
- When you sense a regular pattern of negative behaviour towards someone else (especially that child in ...), it may well be time to check on what you are saying to yourself about that person.
- When stressful events occur in your life, it can be helpful to tune in to what you are saying to yourself about those events.

Be fair dinkum in disputing and reassessing self-talk. Make it a habit.

Take, for example, the case of 'Bruce' and say: 'OK, I'm really annoyed that I mucked up. It was silly. I forgot the work sheets for the students — maybe I should have remembered,

but I didn't, I ran late. Next time I can ... and it's natural I'll feel put out. So I'm human, I'm fallible. I don't need to indoctrinate myself with failure!'
- What can you learn from this?
- How could you deal with it at the time? (Explain to the VP, apologise to the class; don't 'crawl', just make a reasonable apology.
- What can you do, actively, to improve in the areas you've failed in? And remember — to fail does not mean you are a failure.

Tuning into self-talk is not easy; it needs to be practised like any skill until it becomes a habit.

We're likely to be using negative self-talk when we're experiencing negative emotions towards someone or some situation. As an exercise, try randomly 'tuning in' to 'hear' what you're saying. For example, when Jason whines at you in class, when your 3-year-old child throws a tantrum, when Jason argues with you, when you're aware that you didn't reach your target, try thinking: 'What am I saying to myself right now?' — catching yourself at it, as it were.

Write down what you were saying to yourself. There's something about capturing what we 'say' on cold, hard paper. It seems to classify and clarify it for us. We can see how stupid, overstated, even irrational are some of the things we say to ourselves. Often we'll only be able to write it down later; at the time, we might just be able to grasp the tenor of it.

Stop, check, dispute, rephrase.
1   What was the situation at the time I got upset?
2   What was I saying to myself about it?
3   What was I feeling?
4   What happened as a result?

The reason for disputing erroneous and self-defeating thinking is that it can bring about a more effective way of coping, both emotionally and practically.
- Are these kinds of thoughts helping me?
- What is the outcome, the consequence, of this kind of thinking?

Even changing expressions such as 'I always', 'I never', 'I can't stand it', 'Nobody here cares', 'Everybody here is ...' is a useful first step. Instead, you can say:

'I sometimes, even often, but ...';
'Some people here are difficult to work with, but ...';
'I can do it when ...';
'It may be difficult, but ...';
'It will get better when ...';
'Even if I fail, I'm still OK as a person'.

Private speech, as Wragg (1989) has noted, has a self-guiding and self-regulatory function. Beliefs, thoughts and deeply held assumptions have a significant effect on emotions, states of mind and behaviour.

Adaptive or maladaptive behaviour is a skill to be learned (even in private thought).

Challenging faulty ideas and beliefs

When we fail, we experience feelings of stupidity and loss of self-esteem. If we add to the failure negative self-talk, we fall into the trap of 'self-downing'. 'It's all my fault; I always screw up!' 'I can't stand it when I fail.' These overgeneralisations are often backed by beliefs such as 'I shouldn't fail', 'I must get it right', 'A good teacher should ...'.

If we don't dispute this rubbish, we'll feel worse than we need to feel. We may lock ourselves into a non-coping rut.

'How does what I did make me a failure?' It doesn't. It shows up your fallibility, skill-deficit, poor planning — but it doesn't make you a failure!

'But I failed on my promotion. It's terrible!' So you failed; of course you feel low, but what can you learn from it? Maybe you haven't been in the job long enough. Maybe you need to do more work on curriculum documents, on being interviewed — whatever. How terrible is it when compared with war, famine, losing your house, losing a limb? It's unpleasant, annoying, temporarily frustrating — but terrible? Accept yourself, with your limitations. Repair and rebuild. Then you'll feel better too.

We all make mistakes and misjudgments, but you're not stupid or worthless, even when you fail.

This kind of *disputational thinking* enables us to:

- stop rating ourselves ('I must be thoroughly competent in order to be worthwhile — if I'm not, I'll feel awful and I won't be able to stand it');
- live with inevitable frustrations — 'the thousand natural shocks that flesh is heir to (*Hamlet*) — and accept the truth of fallibility (in self and others) while working for improvement;
- resist the stupid demands that things 'must be ...' when clearly they are not;
- evaluate difficult and normally stressful events as difficult, annoying or inconvenient rather than terrible and catastrophic.

Further, disputational thinking makes it possible to use the energy and emotion of worry to constructively attack the problem and rebuild.

If we do that, we use the energy as concern — not merely as fruitless worry. If we *just* worry, we're allowing the problem to assume a disproportionate dimension. Also, when we worry we often invest a lot of emotional energy in two areas that we are not technically 'living' in: the past and the future.

As Jesus said, 'Therefore do not worry about tomorrow, for tomorrow will worry about itself. Each day has enough trouble of its own' (Matthew 6). Tomorrow does not belong to us, it is not here yet. Plan ahead, do what needs to be or can be done, and then keep living *today*. Of course Jesus said much more about this aspect of worry, but you can read that for yourself. The meaning and purpose of living is not per se the focus of this book.

Learn to replace one's psychological junk mail with realistic and optimistic ideas and attitudes, as well as to evaluate and dispute it. Exploring the place of attitudes, beliefs and assumptive frameworks through peer support can help to refocus what is important, what is valuable in balance with your role, work and relationships.

How do you explain events to yourself?

Martin Seligman's research into 'learned helplessness' supports the view that the way we explain the things that happen to us may be as important as what actually happens. Also, the characteristic way we explain things also has implications for one's mental and physical health. Seligman calls this our 'explanatory style' — people have a characteristic way of explaining reality as 'bad', 'awful', 'always being ...' when it is often ambiguous.

The revised helplessness theory says that people have a characteristic way of explaining bad events when reality is ambiguous. They explain events as being caused by something stable or unstable, global or specific, internal or external. If your relationship breaks up, for example, you can come up with a variety of reasons. If you explain it as something that is stable over time ('I always screw up my personal relationships'), you will expect it to happen again and will show signs of helplessness in future relationships. If you explain it as global rather than specific ('I'm incapable of doing anything right'), you will expect bad things to happen in all areas of your life and feel even more helpless. If you explain it as internal rather than external ('It was all my fault, I did everything possible to keep the relationship going'), you are likely to show signs of lowered self-esteem.

According to Seligman's revised helplessness theory, a person who tends to explain the bad things in stable, global and internal terms ('It's going to last forever, it's going to affect everything I do and it's all my fault') is most at risk of experiencing depression when bad events occur.

Trotter, p. 32

In a peer-support program I was working with a quite stressed colleague in his class. He repeatedly said: 'Look, they're out of their tree — they're bloody animals! I can't stand it. They never listen to me!'.

Sure enough, as I watched him teach (and he had problems — they were a tough class), I could see his tenseness, his stress. Afterwards he said: 'See? I told you, I told you, didn't I? They always muck up'.

We reversed roles with the same class and although they were difficult for me too, I perceived that we'd had a reasonable lesson. He couldn't see it. 'They *always* muck up.'

Alex

David is a secondary science teacher. He describes the process he went through over a twelve-month period with peer support.

I've had some problems with quite inappropriate emotions and classroom discipline. I was experiencing excessive frustration, anger and even anxiety at various times.

Thankfully, my classes are no longer places where heated confrontations are common. I've learned a number of things in this last twelve months that have changed my thinking, teaching and discipline.

1 My 'beliefs' were causing my stress. I used to say 'I'm hopeless' — rating myself. I used to demand obedience ('you should obey me'). I used to insist on 'winning' ('I must win in my discipline').

I've since adopted more reasonable 'beliefs'.

2 I've begun to understand the goals of behaviour — why children seek attention and power. This has helped me to see it's not all personal (against me) and it's helped me to plan my discipline so that it's more effective. I no longer see myself as the 'victim', the students can't simply make me upset; I too have a contribution to make.

3 In my discipline, I've moved from a more control/punishment perspective to try to develop self-control and respect for rights in my students. I now think about my actions in discipline situations, and plan for when I have to discipline. In this I am able to respond rather than react. My pupils also grow through making choices about both their behaviour and its consequences.

4 I've used clear, fair rules and consequences with my students and I have less conflict; the rights of both teacher and pupil are now protected by these rules, stated clearly and positively. The rules derive from commonly accepted values such as human worth, co-operation, communication and self-direction.

5 Lastly, peer support has really helped. I have listened to my peers, their ideas and advice; they have especially helped when I've had to use time-out procedures.

In summary, my stress level is more under control because I have adopted new beliefs and new practices. I've been able to reassess my teaching skills by using a peer-support scheme and learning to take a middle path — one of being assertive, actively resolving conflict with thorough planning, not swinging 'wildly' from one extreme to the other — from passively giving in to students to actively confronting them.

David

Instead of struggling along alone, David took steps with peer support to change his situation.

Failure

The Chinese ideogram for crisis apparently contains characters for both 'opportunity' and 'danger'.

Fail meaningfully!

Learn from a mistake, but first know and see the mistake for what it is — a mistake. Label it as such, and ask: 'How can I do better next time? What will I need to do? What support and help do I need? Who can give it?'. We can learn as much from what did not work as from what did.

Relabel the stress of failure

'OK, I did that; it was dumb. But I'm still all right [self-esteem]. Now, how can I do it better next time? Failure is normal, useful, natural — even healthy, provided that we use it; it can access both where my strengths and limitations lie. Provided that I am honest with myself about the failure — even a significant failure — and then redirect the emotional energy into the future, I'll feel less depressed, more optimistic.'

Seek support

Of course, you may well need support to do this, and that's not easy to ask for — to say: 'Look, I did this ... I really messed this up ... I need to talk about it'. The perspective and support of people we trust can boost confidence in redirecting our failure. This is why a supportive school environment legitimises natural failure and can tolerate even the 'dumb' mistakes (as well as the honest ones!), but emphasises supportive problem ownership. No problem (including failure) is so bad that we can't talk about it to someone; no problem is so bad that something cannot, in time, be done about it.

'Next time'

After a lousy day (when you arrived late to your class, a colleague was rude to you and the class didn't go well), it's easy, even natural to blame either yourself or others. 'I should have said ...!' 'Why did I (or didn't I) set the alarm? Prepare those sheets? Check which room I had for 8D?'

If our self-talk ends there, it often falls into replay mode; we go over the same negative, useless phrases. One deceptively simple tool that has helped me is to put in the phrase, 'Well, *next time* I can ...' or 'Even if I was wrong or stupid, *next time* ...'.

This stops the downward spiral, while acknowledging our faults and others. It also redirects our thinking towards how we could do better next time. It generates new options, with peer support generating some solutions to 'the problem', and can result in a less stressful occasion next time the same thing happens. It puts our failure, the 'bad event', into perspective.

As Joseph Schwartz, a sociologist at New York State University, writes:

Job demands are potential sources of stress, but how much freedom a worker has in deciding how to meet those demands will determine if they actually produce stress. One way to lessen stress is to talk things over with fellow workers in similar jobs, try to identify the problems and formulate constructive alternatives. Then set up meetings with management and develop alternative job designs ... taking joint action leads to a feeling of involvement and efficiency among workers.

Psychology Today, April 1989, pp. 18–19.

What Schwartz and Karasek outline is the essence of peer support — the model that is referred to regularly in this book as the necessary process for more effectively managing personal and organisational stress.

With peer support (from my colleagues, faculty head and even the principal!) I've felt better — like it's not all my fault when things go wrong. It helps me to put my problems in perspective and takes off me the pressure of thinking I'm the one totally responsible for it all. But even a few years back I couldn't have shared my feelings or concerns (especially as a male) for fear it would be seen as a weakness or even a black mark against me!

Don

Peer support for teachers

I wish I had known a few of these techniques (on classroom discipline and management) a few years ago when I very nearly joined the stress statistics, due to trying to handle a very tough class using the 'power-struggle' approach. I was also too proud and too naive to attempt to discuss my problems with any of my colleagues, who seemed to be handling things so well.

Anthony

I can remember the good years by the teachers who worked opposite me. I didn't want them to fix up, tell off or counsel the difficult students I sent across now and then — I just wanted support.

Joy

An isolated culture?

Traditionally, teachers have tended to work and operate as professional isolates, diving into the staff room for a cuppa or a smoke (though that's not on now, fortunately) to revitalise, then darting off when the bell goes — or earlier — for last-minute photocopying.

In a structured environment such as a school, where we work so close to one another (spatially), it's ironic that we perpetrate a culture of 'social separateness'. Sadly, this characteristic extends to problem sharing or solving, where admission that a problem or need exists is confused with 'professionalism' and a loss of self-esteem. If I admit that I can't really manage 8D, it appears (in some teacher's minds) to signal failure, admission of incompetence, inability to cope, 'It'll be recorded on my file', 'What about the senior teacher's mark?'.

Teachers have tended to stay out of each other's classrooms and not talk about their own discipline problems. Too often teachers do not seek help because it feels like an admission of incompetence and they do not offer it because it feels like accusing a colleague of incompetence. As a result, the tradition of classroom isolation persists in many schools.

Elton Report, p. 69

Adapted from 'Punch' 11/1/84   W. A. Rogers.

It is this very culture of reluctance and isolation that feeds the stress dynamic. Research shows quite clearly that we all need a fundamental sense of social support: the feeling that we are understood, listened to; that we have backup; that it is all right — here — to ask for help, talk about one's problems and contribute to decisions that significantly affect them (timetables, duty rosters, class groupings).

When the pressure is on — when we feel we're not coping — there is a tendency to draw back, to 'isolate'. This is more prevalent in a school that perpetrates the keep-it-to-yourself mentality. It creates, in the isolate, an impression that others don't care or wouldn't understand. This further increases the feeling of psychological discomfort and hence the withdrawal: staying in the classroom, making only essential appearances in the staff room, lunching alone, say nothing that is not essential.

Others, of course, may want to care, but either don't know how to get through or, if rebuffed, feel they cannot effectively offer support. Communication breaks down, and the result is lack of mutual trust and apprehension.

Building a supportive culture

Chris Kyriacou, a noted researcher on teacher stress, indicates (1981) that 'the degree of social support available in a school is a crucial factor in mitigating stress'.

Kahn and Katz (1960) in Rutter (1979) have found that supervisors in highly productive working groups were generally felt by employees to be supportive, understanding of difficulties, concerned about their problems and needs and, most importantly, interested in them as individuals.

While this research is not directly drawn from a school, Rutter makes the point that investigations of supportive climates in other institutions suggested that people 'work and behave better when they are well looked after and feel that those in charge understand and respond to their personal needs'.

While this might sound pedestrian to some, it is an essential feature of any level of management.

Staff need to feel and know that they are supported and will be listened to with respect concerning their needs. School leaders are halfway there when they make the creation of a supportive school environment a primary goal. Teachers with supportive supervisors do not feel the same 'role strains' as those without, even if their roles are ambiguous.

Reducing occupational stress in the workplace involves a number of things:
- occupational and environmental support;
- development of discipline and management skills;
- skills in organising time and workload;
- personal-coping skills.

These factors, however, will be less effective without a *culture of peer support*.

There is at present a program in schools that enables students to develop personal assertive skills to handle intimidation or abuse from others. Among the things we say to students in this program are these:
- 'Nothing is so bad that it can't be talked about or shared';
- 'No problem is so big or difficult or insurmountable that something can't be done about it'.

If we can say this to children, can we not encourage a climate like this in the workplace? We are encouraging not bleeding hearts, but a reasonable, supportive culture.

The role of senior staff

Senior staff can do a lot. While ad hoc support, of necessity, occurs in a school, endorsing a 'culture' of support from senior staff can facilitate the process. We cannot *make* staff support one another — that would clearly be counterproductive — but we can use formal or semiformal approaches and encourage the less formal approaches by modelling and inviting support.

Many strategies are possible, including:
- year-level meetings to share issues of concern, especially about difficult students;
- cross-faculty meetings;
- team-teaching opportunities;
- use of staff meeting times in small, mixed-ability groups, section meetings, problem/ task analysis groups;
- special staff-forum times with small-group opportunities;

- invitations to set up small, collegial support groupings across the school.

Most importantly, teachers need the assurance that when significant issues arise (such as high-level disruptive behaviour or hostile and unsafe student behaviour) they will be given support without imputation of failure.

One of the schools I worked in as a teacher-consultant had several high 'reputation' students and one or two 'reputation' classes. At the beginning of the year it was clear that a lot of whingeing and complaining had had little effect. We went for a support approach, inviting all those who taught 'Craig' to meet for a group discussion. Such groups need skilful and thoughtful direction; they need people who can invite the quieter, more reticent and democratic to tune in and redirect the louder or more cynical, and senior staff need to give careful thought as to who on their staff have this skill.

One of the first-year teachers shared, with some emotion, the way he felt when Craig was in the class. 'I just don't know what to do. I couldn't believe how rude and foul his language was — all I asked him to do was to go back to his seat!' To his credit, one of the more senior staff admitted that he too had problems with Craig. 'You too!' The first-year teacher had bottled up the 'Craig problem' for weeks, believing it was particularly his problem, but joint admission became the starting point for problem discussion and problem resolution.

Despite the resident cynic (the one, as Oscar Wilde said, 'who knows the price of everything, and the value of nothing'), we were able to plan several things even at that first meeting.

- We clarified the nature of Craig's behaviour (especially the impulsive, argumentative behaviour, sometimes accompanied by swearing).
- We discussed the different approaches we were currently using, identifying what clearly was not working and examining why a few strategies *were* working.
- We developed a basic discipline plan that was assertive in nature and not unnecessarily confrontational.
- We also developed a clear time-out plan that included a cue-card system for directing Craig out of the classroom when he refused to leave. This involved sending a 'card' (with the room number on it) to one of various allocated persons, who would then come and escort Craig from the room to a classroom or the office of the year-level co-ordinator.

That meeting evolved into several others (elective and invitational — cynics don't always attend!), where we explored various possibilities.

Assisting Craig to modify his behaviour

We discussed how we could develop a more effective 'contractual' basis for Craig, where key staff members would be willing to assist him with behaviour-change strategies to enable him to be more successful in class (see Wragg, 1989). This contract-phase (over several sessions) was later discussed with Craig, to give a sense of ownership. It specified a few simple goals, especially anger management. It helped him to identify situations in which he was getting himself angry and showed how he could tune in and reduce his intensity of feeling; how he could predict the consequences of 'going down one path'; how he could give himself more positive, helpful messages (self-talk). It did improve Craig's behaviour over the term. He did not become a model student — students like Craig have a history of emotional baggage; what it did do was to reduce everyone's stress, because we had a known and shared problem and were working on the solution supportively.

Improving our own perceptions and self-talk under stress

It was clear that a number of teachers in that group (in the school) had quite self-defeating perceptions, expressed in such statements as 'I'll *never* be able to manage Craig', 'I *always* get angry!', 'He *shouldn't* be rude!', 'I can't stand it when he ... !'. The problem initially was that these working beliefs were quite characteristic for some of the teachers, leading them into self-defeating behaviours in the classroom — for instance, sarcasm, using loud public reprimands, frequent criticism and rare praise (difficult with Craig), argument after argument and useless threats instead of clear choice/consequence approaches.

Modelling discipline skills
We even role-modelled, to one another, some of the discipline skills we'd found to be helpful with disturbed and disturbing students, especially the use of directional language: directing the student aside from the group for a brief rule-reminder; giving simple 'choices'; redirecting instead of arguing; making assertive statements when we were angry or had been put down or verbally abused (this is something we never ignore, though we do *tactically* ignore petulance, sulking and dumb insolence.

Using teacher support
We discussed how we could better use our colleagues in exit/time-out strategies with difficult students and how, as subject teachers, we could more effectively follow these instances up. No teacher wants the unneccessary, ridiculous and stressful situation of a Brett persistently screaming his lungs out, a Shane kicking cupboards or climbing walls, or a Craig or Melissa verbally abusing other students or the teacher. If students have been given reasonable opportunities (non-confrontationally, but assertively) to own their behaviour, teachers need exit, time-out and follow-up support in dealing with them.

Peer coaching
Later we explored peer coaching as a means of improving our repertoire of skills, and this too was a totally elective process (see pp. 104 ff).

The senior staff endorsed this supportive process and it was taken up more widely across the school, especially with first-year teachers. Many of the ideas were later included in the school's discipline policy; for example:
- the need for each teacher to have a clear discipline plan (see Fig. 4.1);
- a clear exit process for disturbing students (who would previously have been directed and redirected, and to whom a non-threatening choice/consequence would have been made clear;
- a clear follow-up process to determine what longer term measures would be necessary (such a follow-up needs to involve both class and subject teacher at some point, so that re-establishment of working relationships can follow).

Another way we use peer-support approaches is to address the issue — to explore the problem or problems — within the group, in terms of 'control'. This includes brainstorming those aspects of a role, task or situation over which we have:
(a) minimal or no control
(b) negotiated control
(c) clear, direct control

It can be useful to list statements in the form of a table, using as headings these three degrees of control. This 'brainstorm and reflect' approach makes possible a clearer *definition* of the problem or issue and a more realistic action plan; the listing and brainstorming process itself gives a feeling of control.

We recently did this with a curriculum issue. The new curriculum at Years 11 and 12 was creating some stress for staff, especially regarding class sizes and appropriate ways of servicing the work-required-assessment model, marking schedules and how to 'meet the guidelines' effectively, and simply how to fit it all in. A number of questions were asked, which the facilitator clarified in terms of control, and a number of common concerns emerged together with solutions and ideas.

We also explored the nature of some teachers' 'beliefs'.
- 'I feel guilty when I fall behind.'
- 'The students are so lazy. They should pull their fingers out!' (But how?)
- 'It's not fair, this damn Year 12 program!'
- 'It's not my job to baby-sit lazy Year 11s and 12s!'

There were some overly demanding, some self-defeating beliefs and language. We explored these, and looked at beliefs and self-talk as something over which we do have direct control. After all, there are some things in teaching over which we may not have direct or full control — student home life, background motivation or IQ, course guidelines and require-ments — but we can have negotiated control over application of the guidelines, structure of the units of work, the way deadline dates and marking are organised and the way we deal with motivation and recalcitrance, preparation and planning time.

The key was the time given to:
- authentic whingeing (our common lot!);
- clarifying 'control';
- bringing some realism into our demands and fears;
- looking actively among our peers for solutions and bringing in support from others either in the school or outside it to help us in our support-planning meetings.

Not another meeting!

We all, naturally, complain about the number of meetings in schools these days, but either peer support can be built *into* our meeting structures or we can build ad hoc groups to actively address issues of concern on use of peer groups for skill development. These can be established on a timeline that suits the participants. I have had many very successful ad hoc meetings over an after-school coffee or wine session.

One way to kick-start a peer-support culture is to have a staff workshop outlining the benefits of a collegial support culture. Examples of successful models within the school's region can be shared (invite speakers from other schools) and outlines given of the way peer support can be used, stressing especially its elective nature. Even where a school is using peer appraisal or 'mentor' schemes for skill-development, it is important that as much choice as possible be offered. Where staff are clearly struggling, a private offer of support (through a mentor) needs to be made and the earlier the better.

Because peer support is linked to staff welfare, a note on it ought to be included in the staff handbook. For instance: 'At this school we take a team approach to discipline and welfare. Therefore teachers are encouraged to share any concerns they have about classroom discipline and to look for appropriate support in developing more effective discipline plans for their classrooms'.

Where peer-support groups are created for skill development and training, they can be a useful adjunct to professional development; however like any support group, they need key facilitators who have human-relations skills and staff credibility, and who are *available* to staff.

The following reasons for peer support were listed by teachers who had made stress-related WorkCare claims (Victoria, 1987).
- We need someone (a 'buddy', maybe) to give less formal information on the unwritten laws of the school.
- We need other teachers at the *same level* with whom to discuss alternative strategies for management and teaching — even to discuss (positively) our failures.
- We need to celebrate our successes — even the small ones (have a pat on the back).

Peer support was seen by these teachers as achieving the following goals.
- We could keep 'sane' instead of just keeping problems to ourselves.
- We could become aware of other points of view and perspectives, listen to others and gain feedback, and learn from others' knowledge and experience (this is a central — even common-sense — axiom often given little weight in some schools).

In this we also learn about ourselves by clarifying our own beliefs and values; we avoid the development of 'tunnel vision'.
- We need to promote peer support as an OK norm — to seek positive feedback and criticism, to help build and maintain confidence and, most of all, to know that someone cares about us as people.

Organisational stress

The work environment

I recall asking for some furniture when I started the year with a Grade 5. 'Oh, there are some old desks in the shed.' 'What?' 'In the shed — the old bike shed.'

Several teachers had got there before me, so I was left with some desks circa 1945. My 11-year-olds had to write on those desks!

If I had been more assertive then, I could have asked for appropriate furniture. I assumed it was the norm, that was the trouble. I was a beginning teacher then.

At the beginning of the year it can be a useful exercise to map out the teaching terrain and note its features: lights (do they all work?), seating, cupboards, resources, doors and windows. Make a list of legitimate concerns and give a copy (signed and including the room number) to your section leader or relevant senior person, with a diplomatic message about the need to have an adequate working environment.

Perhaps you are:
- sharing a phone with twenty other teachers;
- sharing a filing cabinet with ten other teachers;
- scrounging for extra chairs or tables that are not scoured and twenty years old!

Maybe you have:
- tiny work-planning areas surrounded by crammed bookshelves;
- no carpet in the classroom, but a wooden floor on which you can hear every scrape of chair and heel;
- not enough and inadequate resources for your science classes;
- poor and inadequate lighting.

Does this sound like a complainant at work? Too right!

Preventative management

I was teaching in a science laboratory recently, and several things made the morning's teaching more stressful than it needed to be: a flickering and noisy fluorescent light, a chalkboard off its rollers, a wooden (and therefore noisy) floor.

Again, teaching in a portable classroom I was faced with bare glass on two sides and barren walls on the others. The simple addition of thick, net curtains could have reduced the glare and heat and the temptation for students to stare at the next uncurtained group in the next portable classroom a few metres away. Both class scenarios were remediable.

- It is essential that school management takes seriously the effect of environment and workplace on stress and occupational wellbeing.

Organisational stress results from the effect on us of the environment we work in. We may have terrible furniture, or not enough of it; crowded conditions (for students and teacher alike); inadequate or poor lighting or heating (I've taught in places where there's plenty of heat but no way to control it, as well as in the sweltering Aussie portable classroom); situational noise; not enough chalkboard or whiteboard space and no bookshelf or filing space — to name a few concerns.

If we are going to reduce unnecessary stress in the workplace with a view to teacher and student welfare, we need to:

1 identify the workplace stressors (with a survey, or small-group discussion via staff meetings);
2 allow staff (and student) input and negotiation on how to improve the working environment and space so that it best serves the school's needs;
3 decide what needs to be modified or changed in order to reduce occupational, environmental and organisational stress;
4 determine what is realistically achievable in both the short and the long term;
5 develop an action plan with key personnel to achieve those aims.

By reducing workplace stress, we act preventatively as well as supportively.

Consider:
- arranging staff levels and ratios in terms of matching, especially for first-year teachers (so that they don't score the hardest classes);
- equalising workloads and responsibilities;
- allowing ample and useful professional staff survey exercises.

Set aside an hour and a half for staff to pursue, as a problem-solving exercise, the issue of organisational stress. Offer a cup of tea and an explanation that this time has been set aside to allow staff to reflect — to identify and examine concerns about workplace stressors. Time will be given to discuss in pairs and in groups of six the ways in which we might address the issues in the short and the long term. Common concerns will clearly come to light, so a weighting will be given in terms of most or least stressful (for instance, regarding workspace, lighting, heating or areas in the school that are overcrowded).

Depending on what arises out of the first meeting and, for example, on size of staff, it may need to be continued with a session on solutions. Use the two, four, six approach in this way.

1 Record personally the factors in the school environment/organisation which you find stressful (perhaps from most to least). Record also how you believe they could be solved in the short and in the long term. (10 minutes)

2 Work in pairs (cross-faculty or cross-department), sharing the above. What is it about x, y or z that stresses your colleagues? Listen and discuss. Do you have anything in common?

    Develop a joint list, recording:
    - the most to the least stressful;
    - what can be done in the short and long terms. (10–15 minutes)

3 Work in a group of six (plus the left-over numbers) and continue the process.
    - Elect a facilitator and a recorder/feedback person.
    - Go round the group recording concerns and factors that are noted as stressful.

4 Meet as a whole group to focus on what small groups have identified. If there is time, the stressors ought to be listed from most to least (and the weighting given), then the suggestions classified according to whether perceived solutions are short- or long-term and what it is important to address quickly.

5 A further meeting will often be needed to:
    - pursue any blocking factors;
    - examine existing structures or features that can augment the change process;
    - allocate key persons or task groups, creating action plans and timelines;
    - nominate a review meeting to assess the action plan for organisational change.

Since the purpose of this process is to pursue the issue of environmental stress, it is important to redirect any other issues that may arise (for example, concerning curriculum or discipline).

In one school with severe limits to funding, the administration team scoured second-hand shops for filing cabinets, seating, bookshelves and so on. The local market produced some cheap pot-plants and the carpet factory some seconds in industrial carpet. Of course, the Ministry of Education *should* have provided all this and more, but you could wait for ever!

The supportive school environment

... it is essential to ask why schools function in the ways that they do, and consider how and by which means they have an impact on the behaviour and attainments of the children they serve.

Michael Rutter, p. 177

Of course, education cannot compensate for the ills and inequalities of society as a whole or of family modelling in particular. However, the major research project (over 15 000 hours) in 1979 of Rutter et al. (p. 181) showed that schools as academic and social institutions can and do have effects on student behaviour and success in learning.

Those effects arise from several key elements:

Collaborative practices

These occur at their best when schools, wherever they are, make a significant effort — school-wide — to inculcate collaborative practices for staff and, where possible, for parents and students. This means allowing and structuring genuine opportunities for staff to contribute to and make decisions that concern key policy areas and practices in the school — especially regarding discipline, student management, curriculum, and student and teacher welfare. In a supportive school environment clear, fair, rights-based discipline practices are also discussed and practised school-wide *within a collegial support framework*. No teacher ought to be left to struggle on alone or in isolation with a hard-case student or 'reputation' class.

As the OECD report shows, an effective school begins with active leadership that can initiate a 'vision' and create a structure for that vision to work itself out in the school.

Non-confrontational style

Effective leadership is marked by a non-confrontational style that has the qualities of decisiveness tempered with the ability to delegate, to listen to and enthuse others, to support and unite the team. It is an impressive possibility.

Autocratic styles often see senior staff refusing to delegate or to make possible effective consultative approaches. Conversely, the indecisive leader is often taking the least line of resistance and is swayed by power cliques; there is a fragmented atmosphere, little sense of direction or purpose and a sense that no one is really in charge (except the DP?).

Positive communication systems

Effective, positive communication systems should be established at the formal level. Staff, parents and students need to know about things that directly affect them and to have some input into decision making. This will depend on the kind of communication processes set up, whether formal or informal.

- How are staff informed and consulted on major issues?
- How are staff meetings run?
- How much opportunity is there for staff, parent or student input in *key* areas such as curriculum, discipline and welfare? (I have worked with a number of schools, for example, who have run joint staff-student workshops to explore issues related to welfare and discipline.) While the leadership team will need to make many decisions affecting the host of persons making up a school community, those decisions will have more effective ownership when input has been given through workable collaboration.

Teachers need to feel that their school has a sense of direction. They also need to feel it can be influenced by their views. (Some head teachers find this balance difficult to strike (Elton Report, p. 91).

Even students ought to be allowed to give input into certain basic areas.

- What are some of the things that you really enjoy at this school and that work well?
- Are there any areas you feel concerned about? Why?
- What improvements or changes can we make? How?

Clarification of roles

Expectations and role-requirements, of both teaching and headship, need to be spelled out and put in with the whole-school aims (see chapter 5).

A sense of community

As the Elton Report (p. 91) outlines: 'The most important characteristic of schools with a positive atmosphere is that pupils, teachers and other staff feel that they are known and valued members of the school community'.

A human being is not one thing among others; things determine each other, but man is ultimately self-determining. What he becomes — within the limits of endowment and environment — he has made out of himself. In the concentration camps, for example, in this living laboratory and on this testing ground, we watched and witnessed some of the comrades behave like swine while others behaved like saints. Man has both potentialities within himself; which one is actualised depends on decisions but not on conditions.

Our generation is realistic, for we have come to know man as he really is. After all, man is that being who has invented the gas chambers of Auschwitz; however, he is also that being who has entered these gas chambers upright, with the Lord's Prayer or the Shema Yisrale on his lips.

Victor Frankl, pp. 212–13

Victor Frankl was professor of logotherapy at the International University (USA) and had experienced three grim years in Auschwitz and other concentration camps in World War 2.

Chapter 3

Teacher stress and classroom management

The emotional pressure of classroom management

When one is under stress, one is under emotional pressure. Nowhere is this more taxing than in classroom-discipline situations

---

Common classroom conflict

I walked into an English class (Year 9). I was early. This being an open-plan school, students often come in early as there is no 'lining-up'; they are there early to 'cruise' (socialise). As I arrived, I spotted — leaning back as far in his chair as possible — a boy wearing an old khaki army jacket, with endomorphic legs in skin-tight jeans (ripped in all the right places) and eating potato chips.

Already he appeared to be sending out signals of 'C'mon, what yer gonna do? Eh?' — that almost instantaneous propagation of frustration occasioned by the detritus of fourteen-odd years of poor parenting, emotional deprivation and poorly developed social skills. As I walked towards him, he leaned back even more (with some aplomb) and negligently began a conversation with a girl on his right.

A decade ago I would have found such behaviour (even before speech was entered into) as 'threatening' to me and my 'status'. My beliefs would probably have been based largely on the perception that he was a threat to such status. How dare he (in my spatial presence!) show disrespect. He *ought* to show respect. I, no doubt, would have blamed my resultant anger on his behaviour.

My emotional response, though, would have been fed by high demands — unrealistic demands. Inflexible demands. Dysfunctional demands. As has been mentioned earlier, simply believing that students *should* respect teachers (rather than desiring or wanting) is itself a stressful belief when reality gives no support to that demand. Self-talk of this kind often leads to:

- dysfunctional emotions — we feel more stressed than we need to; and
- dysfunctional behaviour — we argue, yell, blame.

33

TEACHER: Get your feet down! Now! And stick those chips into the bag — now! (*the student doesn't move*). I said now!

STUDENT: Why should I? Not doing anything wrong!

TEACHER: Don't you argue with me! I said get your feet down now and I meant it!

By now everyone is looking on. The student, whose 'goal' is basically power ('I will win; I'll prove I'm more powerful than him') cannot afford to back down. He tap-dances on.

STUDENT: What you picking on me for? The girls eat in class — no, you don't say nothing to them, the sucks!

TEACHER: How dare you tell me what I do or don't do. If you don't move now you are out — out, do you hear!

STUDENT: It's a shit class anyway.

TEACHER: Right!! Get out! Now go on!

STUDENT: Why should I?!

Deeper and deeper into the manure it goes.

Controlling belief

The teacher *believes* so much in control ('I must control him') that on meeting intransigence the belief creates a pattern of behaviour that is dysfunctional. Demanding belief, demanding teacher behaviour and emotions coalesce quickly. The belief is not considered at the point of conflict; it is part of the reactive response. So well entrenched is the demand that when reality refuses to meet it, reality is blamed. The teacher is then in a position to move easily towards saying 'He *made* me angry when he refused (argued, challenged, swore, baited, sulked or whatever)'.

Of course, emotional responses are linked to conditions 'out-there' in our environment, but the degree to which they overly distress and disturb us depends on the perception and beliefs we currently hold about such events.

When we overdemand ('he must obey'), our emotions receive a powerful kickback effect from the characteristic beliefs we hold about the stressful event. Of course, in reality we cannot simply *make* the student do anything. We can direct, remind, ask, request, beg, plead, argue, but we cannot make or control.

This does not mean we cannot effectively deal with such behavioural contretemps. Far from it. It does mean that one kind of belief will create more stress than another kind. Flexible, realistic beliefs and appropriate skills can give us a less stressful and more positive style of discipline.

Let's say that I approach such a situation differently, believing that:
- this student and his behaviour present no direct threat (as such) to me;
- his behaviour is his problem — my behaviour is mine, as is my emotion, which is frustration (naturally, I don't deny it — I recognise and use it);
- I cannot simply *make* him put his feet down (if I were to push his feet off, with accompanying aggro, he'd go right off — naturally, and if I plead, or try to reason or bargain, he'll argue back);
- he cannot simply *make* me upset, even if he swears (while it's really annoying, rude, stupid behaviour, I'm OK despite that);
- I'll stick to my plan (take a few relaxing breaths, remember what to say when *in* the conflict, and go into it).

Of course, if I fail, I fail in the trying of the plan. This does not mean I am a failure. One of the unfortunate aspects of 'emotional reasoning' (Burns 1989) is that we assume our negative emotions reflect simply the way things really are. I feel an 'absolute' failure because

I botched that class. 'I must be a failure' or 'I am a failure' — there is a big difference between using the present tense to define, 'am', and using the past tense, to say 'I have failed in this instance'. One is global definition, the other specific — and the kind of self-talk used will affect the degree of stressful emotion we experience.

In chapter 2, peer-support approaches were discussed to provide the necessary emotional, practical backup and support for extra hard cases. In this chapter, classroom-management strategies are explored further to help support a more conscious, personal managing of stress in discipline situations.

The unconditionality and rigidity of belief about the activating stressors creates the stress *as much* as does the rotten kid, the punishing grade, the difficult grade, the difficult school, lousy buildings, timetables that seem unfair and so on. We can (and should) work at changing and modifying structures where possible; even where we cannot, we are still left with what and how we *choose to believe* about the stressors.

Choosing our thinking?

The use of the word 'choose' is deliberate. Often we sustain negative/dysfunctional emotional stress because of the beliefs we hold — demanding and absolutistic (children must obey their teachers, 'I can't stand that kid', children must not swear). Sustained, negative emotional stress makes it very difficult for us, as teachers, to achieve our goals of effective teaching and classroom management.

> For if sustained negative emotion results from your own thinking, you have a choice as to what you can think and how you can emote. That remains one of the main advantages of your humanness: you can choose, usually, to think one thing or another; and if you make your goal living and enjoying, one kind of thinking will aid this goal while another kind of thinking (and emoting) will sabotage it. Naturally, therefore, you'd better pick the first rather than the second kind of thinking.
>
> Ellis & Harper, p. 33

As Bernard and Joyce (1985, p. 355) point out: 'We believe that most psychosocial stress derives from the manner in which the individual interprets and appraises a situation'.

Emotional habits

I know what I feel when things don't go the way I want or demand. I've felt, on occasions, like leaping three desks and maiming that rude, annoying, persistently disruptive student. I also know that I can't simply make him shut up, and on reflection might even agree that my beliefs and actions are unhelpful. The problem is finding a *balance* between what I know (on reflection) to be dysfunctional practice and what happens in the situations I find too stressful in my teaching practice.

Effective change involves changing emotional habits, thinking patterns and behaviour. Maultsby (1977) describes the process as one of conscious conversion: 'Converting practice means converting your old involuntary emotional habits back to their original voluntary state'. We can't stop the emotions from coming and it's dangerous to suppress or ignore them, or pretend they don't exist (deny them). It is healthier, less stressful to acknowledge them and learn to voluntarily manage them at the point of recognition. This takes effort and practice. I cannot choose my emotion, but I can choose my perceptions.

- Imagine yourself faced with a situation that creates frustration.
- Try to work out what you could be saying to yourself about the situation and your response.
- Re-imagine the same situation with a new thinking pattern.
- Develop an action plan that addresses beliefs, legitimate emotion and more effective ways (discipline skills) of dealing with the issue.
- Discuss stressful scenarios with peers to utilise emotional and professional support in problem solving and change.

Cognitive rehearsal

W.A Rogers

Conscious discipline

Going back to the boy with the feet up and what I actually did. As I approached him I was consciously relaxing my body (no pointed finger or tense shoulders) to demonstrate that he was no threat, keeping a slow, upright walk until, about a metre from him, I simply said: 'G'day, my name's Bill Rogers, what's yours?'. I said this pleasantly, expectantly, hand outstretched. No crawling, no sycophancy. Just expecting respect. I was also saying to myself, 'You can do it, he's no threat'. He took my hand (feet still up, chips on the table) and muttered, with oblique eye-contact, 'Gavin'.

'I'll be taking the class for English today. We'll be starting in a sec.' As I turned to walk away, I added as an aside, 'Feet down, thanks, Gavin', and walked away as though I knew he'd do it. I didn't stay to ram it home or 'overdwell' (Kounin 1971) by moralising or preaching. I was trying to communicate; I wanted him to own his own behaviour. As I made my way to the whiteboard I noticed, out of the corner of my eye, that he slowly (oh, so slowly) put his feet down, but carried on eating the chips, grinning.

My 'verbal discipline' was, in tone, relaxed, almost off the cuff, but it was also *conscious* and part of my cognitive plan.

I have found that it is stress-reducing to have a prepared verbal repertoire for common disruptive situations. This gives a sense of being prepared, which increases one's confidence — I have referred elsewhere to the concept of a discipline or management plan (Rogers 1989, 1990). As I acted this way, I felt less stressed by the event.

Later in the lesson, the potato chips reappeared. I casually walked over during the on-task assistance time, and said: 'I like potato chips too, but it's a class rule, Gavin. I want you to put them in your bag, thanks, or on my desk'.

Again this was conscious — a simple direction to desired behaviour, with an 'I' message: 'I want you to ...'. I implied a choice, 'in the bag or on my desk', rather than merely snatching them off. They're his, after all.

It proceeded something like this.

STUDENT: Geez, they're only chips!

TEACHER: I know they are (*tune-in*) but I want you to put them in your bag or on my desk, thanks, Gavin (*redirection*).

STUDENT: C'mon, I didn't eat at recess, did I? (*his avoidance game*)

TEACHER: 'Maybe you didn't (*tune-in*) but you know the rule; in your bag or on my desk, thanks, Gavin (*redirection*).

STUDENT: (*folding his arms, sighing and pouting*) I'm allowed to in other classes!

TEACHER: Maybe you are, (*tune-in*) but the rule's clear, Gavin — (*redirection*) in the bag or on my desk.

At this point I walked away, leaving the behaviour under his ownership, as it were, and demonstrating that I expected his compliance with my fair direction and the fair rule. If he had continued to eat, the choice/consequence would have been made clear to him (a 'choice' within the fair rules).

How do I feel during this exchange?
Annoyed, but not angry. Why? I'm saying to myself: 'Stick to your plan'. I've even got a cognitive hierarchy of things I can say — a discipline plan that has a prepared verbal repertoire so that I don't just involuntarily respond emotionally. I've imagined these typical situations and planned ahead as far as one can. I've imagined myself facing such behaviours, acknowledging that I'll feel some frustration and then rehearsing: 'OK, I feel frustrated — it's normal. What do I need to say and do in these sorts of situations? If I need to show anger, how best can I communicate it? What sorts of things can I say?'

I know how I used to feel
I used to feel worse, and feel it more often. I used to get significantly more angry because such student behaviour appeared (to my perception of things) to *create* my anger. At least, I rationalised it that way. This *involuntary* cycle made the goal of effective management more difficult to reach. These days I feel better, my skills have improved, and both my relationships with students and my teaching are more effective.

In our peer-support groups we discuss the sorts of situations in teaching that elicit high emotion. We also discuss what we believe we might be saying to ourselves in such situations, and how we act or react. We then discuss attitudes, ideas and perceptions that are dysfunctional, along with a skills program to augment stress reduction.

Anger-creating assumptions about the discipline of children
Having discussed anger, discipline and stress with countless teachers, I see that there is clearly a significant effect on emotion and functional behaviour when certain beliefs are held as reference points. Such beliefs are firmly held, fundamental assumptions about the nature of relationships in the teaching (and, we could add, parenting) context.

I have adapted the following points from Hauk (1967) in Bernard and Joyce (1984) and Bernard (1991). All refer to demand rather than to realistic preference.

Children must not question or disagree with their teachers or superiors.
Clearly they do, both at school and at home. The disagreeing may be either minor or significant; the point is that reality attests it occurs! 'Religiously' believing it must not (when,

in fact, it does) creates my stress, lifts the Richter scale register of human disturbance and sees me arguing, blaming or fighting. Dreikurs et al. (1968) has shown that children today clearly believe they are our social equals and will not merely be *told*, as they used to be. They do question, challenge, even argue. Conversely, they need guidance and discipline based on reasonable behaviour-ownership that includes a leadership style based on respect with appropriate firmness.

Children must be in a position subordinate to their elders, especially their teachers. (sub — below, ordinate — to establish: placed in a position below me)

In the past this philosophy excused some appalling teacher behaviours — the concept (and practice) being that the power (or ordinal) relationship licensed the behaviour. Even with the abolition of corporal punishment, we still see teachers acting on this 'power' belief, as though we have to show who is boss. Treating children as *social* equals does not mean we cannot *lead* them to balance rights/responsibilities and co-operation. We need to discuss the meaning of power and social position; children still want leaders, but democratic leaders who will treat them respectfully, even assertively, with humanity.

A child and his behaviour are the same.

Clearly they are not. Few of us would want to be treated as though that were true. Effective managers address a person's behaviour rather than attacking the person.

Punishment, guilt, fear, blame and criticism are effective methods of child management. We can punish out of anger.

Well, this is 'true'. Approaches based on anger-punishment may be effective, but in doing what? Stopping the behaviour? Immediately? Yes, sometimes it does. But at what cost? Some say it doesn't matter: use *whatever* to teach them that they must not disobey. Effective managers consider the longer term outcomes of behaviour-ownership and self-control. Guilt, fear and put-downs may satisfy the punisher, but they gum up respectful discipline and the human relationship within which management and discipline can work.

Children learn more from what the teacher/superior says than from what that person does.

Clearly, some people don't hear what they say or how they say it or when they say it. Hence, they give a mixed message ('You're just like your —— father!', 'You never listen!', 'You're always late — I'm sick and tired of ...').

Teachers can control their students, can make them do as they are told (they must do as they are told). 'What if they don't?' 'But they should!' 'But some don't.' 'But they should!'

I cannot simply control others by demand (unless, in a fight, I have a bigger, quicker fist or gun and both opportunity and advantage). I cannot control a three-year-old, let alone a teenager. I can ask, request, direct, remind, encourage, beg, plead, grovel, demand — clearly, I cannot *make*. The only people who will be *made* to do things are the naturally co-operative or compliant ones, and many students today are not acquiescent or compliant. Effective managers make rules *with* (as well as *for*) students; they lead by example (even when appropriately angry) and modelling; they show active respect (even to those they dislike) and plan an effective verbal repertoire for discipline transactions so that they can lead, guide, encourage, remind and assert self-control.

We must blame the children; we must make them suffer.

As Jane Nelsen (1987, p. 14) notes:

> Where did we ever get the crazy idea that in order to make children do better, first we have to make them feel worse? Think of the last time you felt humiliated or treated unfairly. Did you feel like co-operating or doing better?

'But shouldn't they suffer? Dammit, it's justice!' A corollary to this is that penalties must hurt a lot if they are to be effective. We can still discipline (lead and guide) without making suffering essential — it may be incidental, but we don't teach self-control by inflicting intentional, purposeful suffering. Children learn best from natural or applied consequences that fit the behaviour and are applied in a context of rights *and* responsibilities — the key right being the right to be treated (even when being disciplined) with respect and fundamental dignity.

Praise spoils the child.
So I'll just yell, nag, blame and whinge. Encouragement for effort does not spoil the child. Think back to the teachers who encouraged you, believed in you, treated you fairly. How did it make you feel and behave?

Children must respect teachers.

Children must earn the respect of teachers.
This is probably the most common stress-creating belief. In the *Independant* newspaper (11 July 1991, p. 2), Afro-Caribbean pupils are cited as being much more likely to be excluded from school because 'teachers think their body language is arrogant and insolent'. It is in the way they 'look at them, walk in an arrogant, exaggerated way, display dumb insolence, look away when challenged ...'.

What does the teacher see? A global set of behaviours indicating disrespect. 'But they should respect their teachers!' 'Why?' 'Because they should!' 'We have status! We're their elders!'

Effective managers don't get unnecessary coronaries by having a cognitive fixation about respect. They desire, invite, model and consequently expect, rather than demand, respect. They also respect (by their actions) children who may (by not being polite, clean and nice) not 'deserve it'. In doing this, they use first names, address the behaviour (assertively, not aggressively), do not crowd personal space, ask to see work ('Can I see your work? Thanks') and do not snatch, pull or poke at it; they treat the student with active courtesy and good humour, not with sycophancy or calculated sarcasm, and they don't hold grudges. If they are angry with a student they address the issue by explaining their anger without going on and on (or putting-the-boot-in), and work at re-establishing good relationships later by helping the student own the consequences of the behaviour and making a better plan for future behaviour, in or out of class. And if they 'blow-it', they apologise and start afresh.

Expressing our anger

Anger is not a disease, with a single cause, it is a process of transaction, a way of communicating. With the possible exception of anger caused by organic abnormalities, most angry episodes are social events. They assume meaning only in terms of the social contracts between participants.

Carol Tavris (1982)

Anger and assertion
Anger episodes

'I can't stand the way he flounces at me! I tell him to go back to his seat when he's clearly time- wasting!'

If you watch this teacher dealing with a student, you see it's not only the out-of-seat behaviour he gets angry about. It's all the other secondary behaviours the student dishes up (Rogers 1991a). The sigh, the folding of arms — closed body language — the sulky and controlled hostility in the tone of voice.

'Look, I said get back to your seat now!' The teacher is stressed. You can see it in his tense shoulders, his pointing, gesticulating, testosterone-charged finger. The tone of his voice is short and bossy. '... and don't you shrug your shoulders at me — all right!' (he is drawn in by the gestural cues as well).

If we could tune in to his self-talk, we'd hear: 'Damn that little ——! Who does he think he is!' There is probably a deeper, more trenchant belief sustaining the momentary (but frequent) outbursts of anger. 'Children must respect their teachers! I can't tolerate their disobedience.'

The student answers back: 'You're always bloody picking on me! I was only getting a pencil — that's no big deal, is it?' Now the teacher is quite angry. Each answering back, each pouting, sulky expression draws the teacher in. Instead of concentrating on the primary issue (being out of a seat), the teacher's belief in win/lose discipline is perceiving all this secondary behaviour as a threat to his status; he takes it all *personally* — his emotion and managerial behaviour are a direct result of these beliefs. Belief outruns any skilled management of the petulant conflict, and he reacts impulsively.

The denouement of this little contretemps has seen the anger come out in aggression rather than in managing and directing the natural 'heat'. Later, he's still stewing over it, re-indoctrinating himself and his anger. 'She *shouldn't* have spoken to me like that! Dammit, the snotty little bitch! Who does she think she is?!' Bottle up our anger — we get sick. Blow it out, uncontrolled, and we may easily alienate others and find we cannot effectively work with them. Communicating our anger means saying *what* we're angry about and *why* we're angry, and then allowing time to cool off, to rebuild and renegotiate later.

We can train ourselves to give a brief holding-time before anger really takes hold as an energising emotion. Count to three or five, and tune in to a prior plan.

Plan for anger episodes

1 Learn to perceive what is happening in anger-arousing situations. Make a note about it: what made you angry, what you think you said, whether you were shouting or bottling your anger up, how physically tense you were. As a bit of detective work, investigate what makes you angry. Set out to *choose* to get angry more productively, even pleasantly.

2 Develop a plan so that next time in *that* situation (traffic jam, rude principal or colleague, sulky and pouting student) you can rephrase what is happening not as awful, terrible and 'I can't stand it', but as difficult, annoying or disturbing, but with your plan, you can manage it.

3 Act from the plan. Make your feelings clear, briefly, simply, without too much heat. *Consciously* stand in as relaxed a manner as possible, remembering that you cannot actually be hurt by what this person says or how it is said. If you are hit (which is unlikely), enrol in a martial arts course next week!

'I don't use that language with you and I don't like it when you speak to me like that. I feel it shows you don't respect me' — this could be said to colleague or student alike.

'I' messages are the simplest form of communicating feelings and concerns. 'I' messages do not set out to judge the other, but to speak freely, purposefully, about our emotion.

4 If you're too angry, withdraw briefly and explain why you are doing so. You cannot effectively resolve much under emotional pressure — later you may be in a position to attack the problem rather than the person. Avoid petulance and simply 'getting back'. Make your goal the workable resolution of the conflict.

5 Be aware of the tenseness in your body. It's a natural arousal, anyway; the body is prepared for — for what? Well, your body won't exactly tell you to punch the stuffing out of x, y or z, even though you may feel like doing it. Your body is telling you 'You're aroused — now do something'.

Consciously pause, count to three as you are aware of the tenseness, and go into your plan. Have a warm bath later, watch a comedy, talk it over with a trusted colleague and plan for a better approach next time.

6 Of course, there is some benefit sometimes in acting angrily even when you're not feeling anger. For instance, when one student puts another down or makes a racist statement.

TEACHER: Damien! (*dropping your voice*) That's a put-down and put-downs hurt.
STUDENT: Yeah, well, you didn't see what she said to me — the bitch.
TEACHER: Maybe I didn't, but *that's* a put down. I'll see you later (*butts in*) see you later. OK, everyone (*the audience*), back to work now.

7 If you blow it, apologise, and not just to earn gold stamps for being a goodie. It's worth it in the relationship-building department, especially with students when you've gone over the top. Keep the apology clear, accurate and non-sycophantic. Explain you were angry at what they did or said, not with them personally. Plan to get angry more effectively next time.

Anger cannot tell us what to do

My tongue seems to get entangled with my brain.
P. G. Wodehouse

Whenever we get overly frustrated or anxious, or feel piqued and angry about something, that emotion seems to take over. We use phrases such as 'I lost my temper', 'I couldn't help getting angry'. Actually, we find our temper rather than lose it, or — to put it another way — we lose it on someone else. Often we cannot stop such emotions coming, but what we do in recognising them (the first step) and in utilising them in personal relationships is another matter. If we cannot learn to effectively *balance* our needs — our wants — with other demands, we will find ourselves unnecessarily forced by others to act against our best interests. Claiming fundamental rights — not to be abused verbally or put down, but to be treated with dignity and respect — are both attitudinal and related to the degree of skill we can exercise when we're feeling uptight, anxious or angry.

It is neither wise nor helpful to say 'I mustn't get angry', 'good people — good teachers — should not get angry'. Clearly, we do get angry. It's a 'natural' emotion — as an emotion. But like all emotions, it doesn't tell us what to do. We need to balance the emotion with judgment and reason to appropriately and authentically communicate our anger. Just letting our anger go, untrammelled, can be quite dangerous, like riding a horse without the necessary reins to lead and guide the energy.

Neither good nor bad

Anger as an emotion is not of itself bad. But it is an emotion, and all emotions need some guidance. We know, for example, that if anger is not resolved in a reasonable way it can lead to bitterness, guilt, resentment or even revenge. It can be a destructive, even dangerous emotion. However, as Conrad Baars (p. 62) points out:

> This does not justify calling anger a 'bad' emotion. What is 'bad' is the failure to do something about the situation which caused the anger, and thereby letting the anger grow into resentment and bitterness.

The point was made earlier that while there are both situations and people that make life difficult, we do bring to situations and relationships certain attitudes and beliefs. The intensity of our resentment, frustration and anger is related to beliefs:
- the broad attitudinal constructs we hold about life, situations and relationships;
- the thoughts we hold at the time of stressful events;
- the thoughts and self-talk we use after the stressful occurrence.

Cognition, behaviour and emotion all interact and affect one another. If I *remain* very angry (or very upset) after an event, I am saying something to myself *about* that event, situation or person.

If I *demand* respect, *demand* that children do not swear, say I *must* be in full control of my class, it is a kind of thinking that will create as much anger as the reality that confirms the opposite of my demand. I cannot *make* reality obey my demand. I can desire, prefer, hope and work for, but a demand is of a different order. Worse, if the unspoken assumption flies in the face of *real* reality, my anger-creating thinking confirms me as a victim. I've worked with many angry teachers who shout, yell, demand and put down, and who would never think of themselves as victims — but they are. They may see assertion as weak: 'I *have* to get angry; those —— deserve it. They should respect me!'. They may even enjoy their anger for a while. The sad truth is that anger-creating philosophies do just that: they create and sustain and legitimise the anger and the resultant behaviour. 'She *made* me angry!' How can we simply be *made* angry by a person? It may well be right and socially just to be angry in some situations, but even then we need to be aware of what we're choosing to do when we use this powerful emotion with any sense of justice.

> The decision of whether or not to express anger rests on what you want to communicate and what you hope to accomplish, and these are not necessarily harmonious goals. You may want to use anger for retaliation and vengeance, or for improving a bad situation, or for restoring your rights. Your goals determine what you should do about anger (Tavris, p. 30).

We could add: 'our values, too'. Getting angry about piddling things such as lateness, lack of equipment, calling out or chewing gum is of a different degree (in terms of rights) from high-level swearing, put-downs, racism, sexism or abuse.

The first step is in seeing such beliefs for what they are: demands rather than preferences. A more realistic pattern of thinking is preferential, enabling us to balance reasonable emotion with behaviour that can assist us to attain our goals. Often quick-responding, angry-style teachers have bad habits — habits of thinking, habits of behaviour, a skill deficit. But habits are learned, and they can be unlearned.

Indecisiveness

The teacher's body posture is not confident; the tone of voice has a softish whine, almost pleading: 'Jason, go back to your seat please'. Or the teacher may start with a foolish question: 'Jason, why are you out of your seat?' with hands open, palm-up, and head to one side — as though, already, he or she knows this is going to develop into an argument. It is as if a chain of secondary behaviours has been invited from the student.

STUDENT: I was just (*with a toss of the head, a sibilant sigh, a pout*) getting a pencil (or 'just checking on the work', or 'I'm not the only one!')

The student will then adopt closed body language (arms folded) and turn the head away to extend the pout.

TEACHER: Jason (*rising inflection*), look, I'm only asking you to go back to your seat. Be reasonable.

STUDENT: I'm not the only one. Geez, what about Melissa and — yeah and — Lisa!

Here Jason folds his arms in a huff, to try to create a diversionary message of 'social justice'.

This will go on until:
- the teacher gets uncharacteristically frustrated;
- the student slopes off, leaving the teacher 'guilty'; or
- the teacher threatens further action and then feels guilty for having been angry.

When the teacher argues from an indecisive stance (as above) or an aggressive, authoritarian stance ('Get back and don't you dare argue with me!'), the outcome is often stressful for teacher and student alike, and time-wasting to boot.

The skill of assertion lies in teaching students (and others) that you will treat them with active respect:
- you will address their behaviour, rather than attack them personally;
- you are not out to win at their expense;
- you are leaving them with a 'choice' — to 'own' their behaviour. We cannot force our will on other people; this is why we use 'choices' within fair rules, and respectful, related consequences when rules are significantly abused.

Assertion

Assertion is the seeking to communicate our fundamental rights in a convincing, clear, firm non-aggressive way: *balancing* our rights or needs with other people's rights and needs. '*How can I do this when I'm under emotional pressure?*' We can only deal with any skill when we address it *as a skill* — something worth learning, especially as a teacher. It rarely comes naturally, but it can be learned. It is needed in discipline and management settings because under pressure it is so easy to fall back on emotional responses alone; this is natural, but nearly always counterproductive.

There are two common responses to pressure.

1 To communicate aggressively by demanding that people do what we want — this often is backed up by a body posture that is tense and a tone of voice that is loud, and may even arise from a desire to hurt, to get back and certainly to show who is boss.

2   To show, by behaviour (tone of voice, body posture, words spoken) that we are deferring to others, even fearful of losing their approval. Certainly, the needs of the non-assertive person are bypassed as the other overrides. This stance is not uncommon in teaching and may come from the strong need to be liked by others.

- 'I don't want to force my will on the students or ...'
- 'I can't tell others what to do. If I do, they may not like me.'
- 'I want — I need — to be respected.'
- 'If I try to be firm, it might not work and I might get angry. A good teacher shouldn't get angry.'

This fear of failure — of losing face or losing control — is reflected in behaviour that may see the teacher becoming a 'doormat' for others.

Access assertion as a skill to be learned, instead of saying 'It's not me! I'm not naturally assertive'. Few of us are. I wasn't, but being male I've had to learn how to make my needs clear in a non-aggressive way and to communicate anger, when it is merited, without riding roughshod over others. I'm getting better at it. It's a skill — practise it.

- Write down the sorts of things you want to say, and rehearse them. Be calm, firm and clear.
- Use an open hand (not a pointing finger) and a firm, clear, voice tone. Stand with the head up, relaxed (not hunched or cowering or 'closed-up'). Keep about a metre's distance, and speak clearly, firmly and directly. Shouting does not convince, nor does the 'I'm being reasonable' nice, quiet monotone.

Address the issue of concern or need without bringing in side issues. For example, say, 'When you call out, I can't hear others. Hands up, thanks', rather than 'I'm sick of you calling out ...'. By including the words 'sick of', we bring in a side issue that deflects the main thrust. When we use a sneering or sarcastic tone, we do the same.

Mixed messages occur when we *intend* to do more than assert our fundamental right or the rights of others whom we, as teachers, have a duty to protect. Aggressive teachers *feed* the aggression in others by what they say and how they say it, and by their tense, vigilant or overbearing body language.

When we model indecisive ('I'm only being reasonable — why can't you, please?'), we may be perceived as wearing a sign saying 'I'm ready to be victimised — go for it!'

- 'David, if you want to ask a question (communicate his need) hands up without calling out, thanks' (express appropriate behaviour).
- Keep eye-contact, speak clearly and firmly.
    'Paul, I want you to stop annoying Jason now and return to your ...'
    'Move away now.'
    'I don't like it when you ...'
    'That's a put-down. I don't like it — stop it, now.'

'I' messages, statements or directions are a safe way of communicating our rights and needs and other's responsibility.

- Avoid arguing. This point has been made several times, but it is fundamental. Arguing, especially in teacher–student situations, is a no-win business. Students have the audience — they'll play to the gallery, and anyway, arguing is based on win/lose conflict models. If the rules are fair and clear, if the consequences are spelled out in advance, if your *aim* is to communicate the student's responsibility, with respect, you've done the very best you can.
- Avoid taking up 'a position' under pressure. It is easy to be sidetracked, so stay on the issue at hand with an assurance that you're prepared to discuss other concerns at another time (but do fulfil this promise later).

Whether in a conferencing, counselling or 'discipline' mode, emphasise that 'we're here to solve *this* problem, not every problem'. In the short term, in class, we use redirective dialogue briefly, but the principle can be extended more widely.

- Focus on the issue of concern.
- Acknowledge side issues by tuning in.
- What's your plan?
- How can I help with that plan?

The teacher moves towards Jason during on-task time in maths. She stands about a metre from him with open hand, confident (not tense) body posture, direct eye-contact — a non-confrontational attitude. All this *already* communicates that there's no threat to the student.

'Jason, I want you to go back to your seat, thanks.' The voice is clear, firm; the tone is expectant without being pushy or sharp.

'Why?!' A smart answer. Jason is in semi-slouch mode, but the teacher is not captured by his body language or tone. She is aware of the 'game' — the 'secondary-behaviour' game (Rogers 1991a).

'The class rule is that we work at our own tables. I want you to go back to your own seat, thanks' (again firm, clear, expectant).

'Look, I'm just discussing me maths with Sean!' (That's untrue; he's been time-wasting, and anyway, in this class discussion occurs within the groups at the tables. He pouts, sighs, folds his arms. The teacher *tactically* ignores this secondary behaviour.

'Maybe you were, but I want you to go back to your seat now, thanks.' At that stage many students will sense they're not getting anywhere, and move off — albeit sulkily. If this happens, the teacher will move away, expecting compliance within the fair rules.

If Jason chooses not to move, or continues to 'choose' to argue, the teacher will leave the choice with him. She knows she cannot literally or simply *make* him move, and she is wise not to get into a pointless argument or negotiation.

'If you choose not to work at your table or seat and keep to our fair rules, you'll be choosing to stay back later to explain *why* you can't do that.' The teacher will then move away, expecting compliance. Again she has been firm, calm, clear — there was no sarcasm, aggro or rancour. The choice is his.

Another approach is to use *question and feedback* to assert the rule or right concerned.

The teacher approaches a student who is eating in class. She could use a direction or 'I' message: 'Jackie, put the chewy in the bin, thanks' or 'I want you to put the chips in your bag or on my desk, thanks'. Simple choice with direction. Instead, she uses a direct question: 'Jackie, what are you doing?'. The question is clear, almost casual. There is no confrontation. To say '*What* are you doing!' would completely miscue the question.

STUDENT: Nothing!

TEACHER: You're eating chips in class. You know our rule. *What are you supposed to be doing*?

STUDENT: Geez! (*with added sulk, pout and snarl*) Miss Snaggs let's us eat in her class, don't she Carla? (*turning to her friend*).

TEACHER: Maybe she does, but what's the school rule?

STUDENT: Dunno!

TEACHER: It's no eating in class. In your bag or on my desk, thanks, Jackie.

Here Jackie mutters 'Shit' and puts the chips away. The teacher moves off to work with another student; she will come back later to assist Jackie when she starts working (to re-establish a positive working relationship), and may keep her back after class for a quick chat, when the audience has gone, to discuss attitude.

By the way, most of the challenging behaviours I'm illustrating occur:
- at the 'establishment' phase of the year, term or group;
- in an unscheduled class;
- in the class taken by a relief teacher.

So, *have a plan* — a plan for a verbal repertoire. Recognise the 'games' you will meet, and prepare ahead. You'll feel better, act more purposefully and still protect the due rights of all.

Write down the sorts of questions (but no 'why' questions) and redirections you might use, and the rule-reminders, and the ways in which you can address argumentative students.

Chapter 4

A discipline plan at the classroom level

A discipline plan is an essential feature of a supportive school environment. The classroom is probably the most important place in the school, in terms of time spent, for teacher and students alike. It is there that the purposes of education are being played out in a fundamental relationship between the teacher-leader and the students. *It is the corporate quality of classroom life that also determines the quality of a school as a whole.* The quality of discipline — its tone and its manner — is dependent on teacher style, planning, consistency of application and support availability.

In their attitude to this, as to any form of leadership, children (and adults) prefer assertion rather than aggression, direction rather than mere telling, choices rather than threats.

Think and plan

- Plan for several clear, fair, 'owned' and enforceable rules.
- Plan for procedures such as monitors' duties, lunch ordering, work requirements, storing of bags, toilet visits, 'seats-away', pencil sharpening and clean-up times.
- Plan how to address disruptive and rule-breaking behaviour in a 'stepwise' approach, from least to most intrusive.
- Plan for consequences that fit misbehaviour (in degrees of seriousness).
- Plan 'exit of student' procedures and the appropriate follow-up.

If a discipline plan is going to be positive, we need to think about how our personal discipline fits in with school-wide aims. How do we establish class rules and routines? What sort of rules are needed? What are they exactly? What are our discipline goals? How will we deal with the 'hard cases'? What backup do we need?

Disciplining students is essentially *leading* or *guiding* them to 'own' their behaviour, to be responsible for it, and do so in a way that respects the rights of others. Effective discipline is not merely the result of good luck or a teacher's personality; it comes from *thinking* about the appropriate skills and from the application of those skills.

1 Establish the class rules at the outset.
These should be few in number, specific, clear, fair and positive where possible.
Cover key areas such as:
- the way we treat one another (be specific — for instance, list five actions of respect);
- how we learn and get assistance for learning (work space, work noise);
- how we solve interpersonal problems in class;
- how we move in around and out of our class;
- how we can feel (and be) safe;
- how we communicate with one another.

For this last, it is better to say, for example, 'hands up without calling out' rather than 'don't call out'. Use language that helps others feel good rather than negative language (see ACER 1991b).

It can be helpful to publish these rules with the children's help, even in picture format — 'our clean-up rule', 'our safety rule' and so on, with bright headings prefacing two or three key points in each rule. Refer to Rogers (1989, 1990) for a detailed exposition of rulemaking. It can also be helpful to have a year-level approach or faculty approach to rulemaking within the school.

2 Discuss consequences of behaviour.
This should be done in such a way that students can see the connection between their behaviour and the outcome of it.

It is important to apply consequences without malice or uncontrolled anger. It can also be useful to have a time-out rule; for example, 'if you make it difficult for others to learn or feel safe, then you will be required to work away from others in the room (to sit away from others in the room — in lower primary, a 3 to 5 minute cool-off time — or to leave the room) until you can come up with a plan to work by our fair rules'. It is important that students know what will happen if they 'choose' to misbehave and that the teacher will be consistent and fair in applying the consequence. The primary message to communicate is: 'you own your own behaviour'. This ought to be discussed as a *school-wide* rule.

3 Have a corrective plan.
Such a plan would deal with calling out, butting in, talking out of turn, classroom wandering, clowning, argumentativeness, pouting, sulking or refusing tasks.

4 Plan the language you will use.
This requires thinking about 'what to say and when'. Write out some positive directions or rule-reminders. Ask yourself: 'How can I communicate a choice? How will I speak to an argumentative or procrastinating student? How will I deal with a student who throws his or her books on the floor in a fit of pique (or worse)?'

- Develop this 'plan' with a grading of least intrusive to most intrusive. Start with a direction, reminder or question, as the context demands, but avoid questions up front in discipline contexts with older students; it invites too much empty discussion (see Fig. 4.1). For example, the question, 'why are you turning around and talking, Denise?' is unhelpful. A *direction* is far better: 'David, I want you to put the ruler down, face the front and listen, thanks', or 'Denise, turn around and face the front. Ta'. Delivered firmly but not aggressively, and with congruent body language, this is much more effective and it does not invite secondary behaviours (such as answering back). If answering back does follow, use the redirective approach (see pp. 37, 45; also Rogers 1989, 1990, 1991a).
- Keep directions and reminders brief and positive, where possible.
    'Sean, Dean, facing the front and listening, thanks'.
    'Hands up, Corey, without finger-clicking, thanks'.
    'Remember to use our rule for ——'.
    'Jason, we've got a rule about ——. Use it, thanks'.

5 Remember the importance of tone.
The effectiveness and positiveness of our discipline revolves around what we say when we're under pressure, and how we say it — the tone we use.

The weighting of a message is not only in the content, although of course that is important; whether in classroom discipline or in interpersonal collegial communication, we need to consider *what* we say. 'I want you to face the front and listen (prefaced by the student's name/s), thanks', is better, more directional, than 'Don't talk when I'm teaching'. But its aim can be affected by *how* it is said. If the tone is demanding, harsh or critical, the *purpose* of the content will not be heard, and if we add to a hard (or sarcastic or demeaning) tone close and gesticulating body language, we convey threat as well as sarcasm, intimidation and so on. If we speak in a tone that is part sigh, part plea, with unsteady eye-contact, shoulders hunched and over-hesitant stance, we may convey the impression that we are 'victims'.

I've had some fun, with many teachers and trainee teachers, experimenting with tone and body language when delivering a message or direction, or dealing with a rude or angry colleague, and clearly quite different messages are conveyed according to tone of voice used and general (and specific) body posture (for instance, pointing a finger, nagging and keeping close). We also learned that we can improve the *congruency* of the messages we give by practice. The aim of assertion, then, in this sense, is to convey your intent clearly and fairly, with due regard to your needs and wants and fundamental rights (dignity, respect, safety) without trampling on those of others.

Intervention model for classroom discipline
(least intrusive to most intrusive)

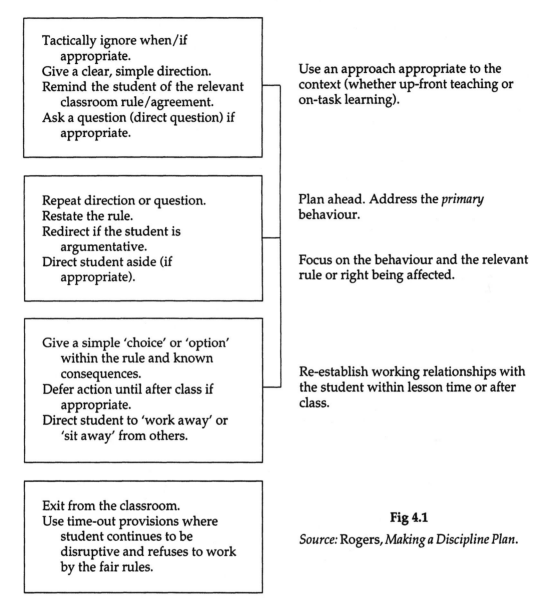

Tactically ignore when/if appropriate.
Give a clear, simple direction.
Remind the student of the relevant classroom rule/agreement.
Ask a question (direct question) if appropriate.

Use an approach appropriate to the context (whether up-front teaching or on-task learning).

Repeat direction or question.
Restate the rule.
Redirect if the student is argumentative.
Direct student aside (if appropriate).

Plan ahead. Address the *primary* behaviour.

Focus on the behaviour and the relevant rule or right being affected.

Give a simple 'choice' or 'option' within the rule and known consequences.
Defer action until after class if appropriate.
Direct student to 'work away' or 'sit away' from others.

Re-establish working relationships with the student within lesson time or after class.

Exit from the classroom.
Use time-out provisions where student continues to be disruptive and refuses to work by the fair rules.

Fig 4.1
Source: Rogers, *Making a Discipline Plan.*

6 **Emphasise positive working relationships.**
Even when you have to correct, isolate or send out, do this with a view to rebuilding a working relationship rather than holding a grudge.

Even smiling, saying 'good morning' or 'good afternoon', encouraging effort and remembering birthdays and saying 'hi' out of class settings will help. Essentially it means starting each day as a new day, and dealing with the students in their (and your) presence.

7 **Have a support and backup plan.**
This is necessary if you are to be prepared to successfully handle:
- the exit of students (to a colleague's room or the vice-principal's office);
- the exit of disturbed or aggressive students refusing to leave voluntarily;

- working with students who are attention-deficit disordered, conduct disordered, socioemotionally disturbed;
- the development of behaviour contracts/agreements.

8 Distinguish between short- and long-term issues in discipline.

Consider an incident involving discipline in which you might direct a student back to her seat: Denise is out of her seat for the third time, gassing away in time-waste mode.

'Denise, I want you to go back to your seat and work there, thanks.'

'Geez! I was just getting a red pen from Carla'. She pouts, arms folded, voice sulky, eyes averted, clearly signalling this message: 'Notice me! I'm in argument mode. Address all my secondary behaviours, not the fact that I'm out of my seat, away from my table'.

'Maybe you were, but I want you to go back to your seat'. Here the teacher moves away as though to say 'it's finished. I expect your reasonable response'. If Denise does not comply, the teacher will give a deferred consequence, expressed as a choice. 'If you continue to ——, you will be choosing to ——. See me later to explain why you won't work by our fair rules'.

All this presumes that the teacher is fair, clear, firm and non-aggressive, but assertive. She doesn't need to get angry on issues like this.

Denise snorts back to her seat, resumes work a few minutes later. Casually the teacher strolls over and re-establishes a working relationship. 'How's it going?' If Denise sulkily says 'I don't want yoo tooo see my work!', the teacher will recognise the goal (attention-seeking — 'Please overservice me by arguing or pleading to see the work') and simply say, 'When you're ready, show me the work'. She will then move off to work with others. In the short-term, under the pressure of the moment and with a class audience that Denise may be 'feeding off', the teacher will concentrate on the primary behaviours and tactically ignore most secondary behaviours unless they are affecting safety or are related to personal abuse.

In the long term, the teacher will have a chat after class to let the student know how she feels. 'In class, when I asked you to ——, this is what you said ...', and the teacher may quickly (but not sarcastically) model the tone of the event so that the student can *see* the behaviour, as it were. The teacher will then add 'I don't speak like that to you, Denise, and I don't like it when you speak like that to me'. 'Sorry!' (Denise folds her arms, still a little sulky.) The teacher's tone here is not sarcastic or get-you-back, it is supportive without pleading for restitution.

If there is time, the teacher may disclose what she believes the student's goal might be. 'Could it be, Denise, that you're trying to show me I can't make you do the work (or obey me) in class? Sometimes at this point you get a knowing look on what Dreikurs (1971) calls a 'recognition reflex'). 'Well, I can't make you'. (It is important, as has already been emphasised, that teachers realise this.) 'I need your co-operation in making a plan to help you do the best you can in our room.'

Put aside time to make a plan or 'behaviour agreement' with the student. Behaviour agreements or 'mutual plans' or 'contracts' (Rogers, 1990, 1991b) need to be supportive, not punitive. We distinguish a contract as a means of assisting students (and teachers — even parents, when feasible) to own their behaviour in responsible ways from consequences, the punitive side of discipline.

In a supportive school environment a head of year, a faculty co-ordinator or even a reference group of key teachers who have expertise in this area will give support to any teacher who believes a contractual approach is a useful adjunct to classroom discipline and its necessary consequences.

Follow-up

Follow-up within a supportive school environment involves applying consequences of discipline, counselling, contracting, imposing sanctions. The purpose extends beyond the immediate application of time-out from the classroom or playground.

- Clarify with the student where and how others' rights were affected by the student's behaviour. Be specific.
- Re-establish a working relationship between the referring teacher and the student (or students).
- Decide — with the student, where possible — what longer term consequences may be necessary (such as reparation or apology).
- Decide whether any formal counselling may be required as an adjunct to consequences. It is important — even with 'at risk' students — to follow through with appropriate consequences as well as appropriate counselling. It is a fallacy to say that we should excuse spitting, throwing dangerous objects, kicking, damaging school property and similar misbehaviour because a child comes from a disturbed setting. While we need to support the child through appropriate counselling and referral, we must also allow the child to experience real-world and certain consequences to teach the power of responsibility and choice.
- Alongside both informal and formal counselling, schools need to provide contractual arrangements for those students whose frequent and intense disruptive behaviour is putting great strain on classroom teachers and students alike.

A classroom discipline plan — what it did for me

- Built confidence in my ability to cope with difficult situations, particularly confrontation with children.
- Provided me with some vital 'tools of the trade' so I feel prepared, not only in my own class, but in the playground and all areas of the school.
- Gave me a set 'pathway' that doesn't depend on external factors such as how far into the term we are, who the child is, etc.
- Defined the problem at hand without being dragged into arguments and secondary behaviours.

- Gave me an important sense of security in the knowledge that I am being fair and consistent in my practices.

Once we have established our classroom rules, the children take a greater responsibility in ensuring their peers abide by them, often without any teacher intervention.

[The plan] released me from an enormous amount of emotional stress every time a problem occurred. Prior to the in-service program on these skills, I came home from school after each day with my Grade 6 feeling shattered. My sole reason for staying there was my determination not to let them beat me. However, once I let the children own their behaviour and accept the consequences for their choices, the atmosphere of the room changed gradually to a point where I didn't internalise the stress their behaviour caused. I was always so intent on maintaining outward calm and detachment, that I carried a lot of stress within me. This made the atmosphere in class negative, which perpetuated the problems.

Some problems still exist, but using the strategies of a discipline plan keeps them in perspective.

Ann, May 1991

Planning — it does save time, and reduce unnecessary stress

An old story: At the edge of the forest, on a rather hot day, a man could be seen stripped to the waist and sweating as he repeatedly hacked away at a tall tree with his axe. He cursed and swore, as the axe made little impression on the hard wood. However hard he swore or hit at the tree, little progress was made. From a distance, another man observed this outpouring of energy upon the tree and thought he could see where the problem lay.

Coming alongside the sweating man, who paused in his work, he said: 'Friend, I see your axe is very blunt; it may be the cause of your problem. Why not stop a while and sharpen it?'

Wiping his brow the other man said: 'Damn it! I haven't got time for all that ...'.

If we make time now for necessary planning, we'll save time later.

It is often that way in teaching. We get so busy, so hemmed in with reports, committee meetings and students to 'follow-up' that we may get a sense of being *so busy*; yet if we were to stop, step back a bit and reorder things, we might just reduce the amount of stress we are experiencing as a result of time and workload pressures.

Nowhere is this more important than in the day-to-day stress of classroom management.

Peer support and preventative management

At any time — but especially at the beginning of the year (the 'establishment phase') — it is important to have in place measures, routines, and practices that prevent unnecessary disruption and enhance classroom 'tone'.

Using team approaches, we've addressed a number of management issues with success — the view being that more often than not someone within the team has had a similar problem, and if there's not yet a solution we will get one together.

The sorts of issues we discuss for preventative management include:
- how we set up and discuss classroom rules and consequences;
- how we can best organise seating;
- how we set up work routines and 'work stations';
- routines for pencil sharpening, handing in (and back) of work (have a tray);
- preparing work for early finishers (extensive work);
- catering for students of mixed abilities;
- how to establish routines for monitors, lunch times, toilet relief and so on.

One peer-support group we had discussed noise level (primary) during on-task time. Many teachers were having problems with the level of student noise, so we got together and discussed the time of day it occurred (mostly after lunch), the particular activities or subject areas involved and what we were currently doing that was or was not working. We then looked for workable strategies and approaches.

Several things occurred as a result: we felt we owned a common problem, we weren't on 'our own' and we came up with several common solutions that worked.

The noise meter

This is a round, cardboard disk with coloured quadrants and a rotating arrow pinned at the centre. The first quadrant is white (for quiet reading time or for up-front teaching when it's 'hands up' or 'one at a time'), the second is green (for working noise), the third amber (for a warning to the class) and the fourth red — this is used when the teacher directs the class to stop, think and remember the working-noise rule. Election of 'noise monitors' in each group (many teachers had group structures) or in each quarter of the room helped to focus on this novelty approach.

If the teacher leaves the arrow on green, it means that she's happy with the level of working noise. The monitor's job is to keep an eye on the meter. If the teacher moves it to amber it acts as a 'privately understood message' to the whole class to stop, think and remember green! The noise monitors use the 'tribal tom-toms' to get the message across to bring the level down. If they succeed, the teacher (without saying anything) puts the arrow back to green. Only if she moves it to red does she need to say: 'Hey, everyone, noise down to green, thanks' (or variations on a firm group direction).

We found that this reduced (not eliminated) group noise in both frequency and intensity. There are, of course, many variations on this theme of cueing, and charts and points can be added with group rewards (now and then) to lift the game. *The point was that we worked on the problem together.* Other teachers suggested bells or flicking a light switch on and off as a non-verbal cue when the noise is too high. All this, of course, presupposes a teacher who can establish a good working relationship with the students and deliver these cues in a good-humoured way. So too with pencil sharpening — a colleague at the meeting suggested having (for a Prep or Grade 1 class) one tin for sharp pencils and one tin for 'to be sharpened' pencils; the children would trade pencils when they needed them.

Toilet routines

Rather than having students coming to ask for permission to leave the room, have a chart marked 'In/Out' and the children's names or, as one colleague had, a chart with twenty-eight nails on each of which hung a yellow triangle with a student's name on it. If children wanted to go to the toilet or have a drink (Prep/Grade 1 composite), Wendy allowed them to take their 'triangle names' and put them on an 'out-of-the-room' nail at the top of the board. When they came back, they put them back on the master board. This taught responsibility and trust, and if children abused the system their names were taken off the board and they had to request permission to leave.

At secondary level a passbook can be used. Record the names (one at a time) and whether in or out; if the system is abused there is a clear record of it, and follow-up can be carried out. This method teaches trust and responsibility.

We have established a number of preventative measures by mutual peer discussion and planning and by actively assisting practices in one another's classrooms:
- up-front, beginning-the-lesson routines;
- finishing-the-lesson routines;
- students' getting the teacher's assistance during a busy class (name on the board? ask three, then ask me? hand up and wait? a desk sign that reads 'help, please', or 'I'm OK');
- effective rostering of class tasks or monitors.

All this is preventative; it can affect classroom 'tone' and reduce unnecessary discipline problems, uncertainty and unnecessary stress. However, principles need to be established during the first sessions with a class, and re-established at the beginning of each term.

My first classroom meeting

My first experience in a classroom meeting occurred in a Grade 5/6, shortly after my arrival at the school, to observe the practice in action as an invited guest. I was very impressed with the concept and felt it would be an excellent way of solving some of the many traumas we were presently experiencing in our Grade 6 class. I was confident because my group were well-practised in conducting class meetings, as they were a regular part of the school routine. This, of course is no earthly reason why a difficult group should magically choose to co-operate and, in fact, the reverse occurred.

Our meeting experienced disorder, featuring 'mob rule' by a group within the class, put-downs, shouting, and disregard for some of the rules or procedures. The usual warm-up activity of touching the person on your right as you say something that you like about them became a punch and put-down, while the chairperson (one designated student, as was the normal procedure) stood on his chair screaming: 'Shut up, you guys!'. The problems brought up were jeered at, solutions offered were inappropriate, and I closed the meeting after fifteen torrid minutes and set the class on writing an evaluation of the meeting, while I did the same (initially to regain my sanity and some quiet in the room).

Following this, I discussed the experience with other teachers and was given immense support and encouragement to persevere, to the extent that a special time was allocated whereby the Supportive School Environment Co-ordinator sat in on the subsequent meetings as chairperson and solved the problem of my being the supposed authority figure with less knowledge or experience than the children themselves. The children were given lots of feedback from the principal and other staff members. The fact that some students didn't want to have class meetings because they found them boring was often discussed. Eventually our meetings were accepted as an important part of school routine that depended on their own input and a balance of humour among the more serious staff!

I've learned the value of:
- having a specific time and place for meetings, preferably not in the classroom;
- using name cards, to be turned over when a person wishes to speak, as the only procedure for talking;
- following a set routine for listing, discussing and offering solutions to problems;
- keeping meetings to a time limit (approximately 20 minutes); and
- the presence of peer support to solve a problem.

Anne

Swearing and stress

It was an English lesson. Towards the end of the lesson I noticed Craig tearing his work into strips, some of which he chewed up and spat onto the surrounding floor and table. He did it calculatingly, purposefully, and he knew that I knew he knew I knew ... a 'hard' man. The late Rudolf Dreikurs would say this student is into power as 'goal' and advise the avoidance of a power struggle at the point where such behaviour is displayed.

Just before the bell went, I directed Craig to stay back. As I let the students out I stood with a hand across the door and firmly but calmly said: 'I want you to clean up the mess over there'. 'Nope! Get your f—— hand from the door!'

As I said, he was a 'hard' man in his own eyes. Although I have a first-Dan black belt degree in tae kwon do, I didn't 'collect' him (though the passing temptation was there).

The first time a student swore at me and told me to 'get f——ed!' I really got angry — quickly, explosively and counterproductively. I can't even recall what I said, because I was so angry that the level of emotion blocked out any useful communication of my anger to the student. I know I yelled and finger-jabbed and threatened and ... I've known male colleagues physically grab, hit or even swear back at such students. Where does their anger come from? Is it justified? Why does such an event create so much stress? I've sat down with many teachers who, well after the event, still recall the swearing with significant emotion. Where does that degree of emotion come from? The words themselves?

Looking back to such incidents, I have noticed in them common elements.

1 Strong beliefs exist — insistent beliefs, such as 'children shouldn't (or mustn't) swear!' and there is the demand that swearing just should not *be* — especially addressed to a teacher. This is an inherent demand in one's status as an adult in a power relationship.

2 There is an inability to distinguish:
  (a) between the social 'wrongness' of swearing as personal abuse and as a lousy 'social skill';
  (b) the natural unpleasantness of swearing, especially the vehement stuff;
  (c) where our own anger is coming from when we're sworn at or when we hear swearing by students who are frustrated or are showing off';
  (d) the more appropriate way to deal with swearing in both short and long terms.

In a number of peer-support groups with teachers we have discussed the swearing issue and concluded that:

- swearing per se has no inherent magic to create the level of disturbance or anger that many teachers experience;
- it is clearly socially appropriate, even beneficial, to display anger of a certain kind in a certain way (we learned a skilled approach to swearing — we learned to get angry assertively);
- you don't change swearing simply by using counteraggression — anger is different from aggression, and can be communicated with appropriate and authentic assertion by those with testosterone as well as those without!;
- swearing (unless it is the low-level frustration kind displayed by a slip of the tongue) should not be ignored, but be dealt with firmly within a school-wide policy.

Identify areas where it is occurring; identify the context and the kind of swearing; agree on common short-term and long-term measures. Swearing itself is not awful and terrible unless we attribute some magic to it. Even hostile swearing cannot in itself make me so angry. I'm not suggesting at all that it is not unpleasant to be called an arsehole! But I can divorce what I hear from the person who delivers it, and I can also express appropriate anger.

If I say to myself 'Children musn't swear!' when they clearly do and did, the lack of congruence between social reality and the demand creates stress as significantly as the event itself. It is unpleasant, but how is it 'awful', 'terrible', 'horrible'? What we believe, character-istically, has an effect on us. When I say: 'Hey, swearing is pathetic, annoying, crude, stupid, unpleasant ...' I'll feel less stressed, especially if (as well) I have a plan for dealing with swearing when it occurs; I'll then act more appropriately and effectively. This cognitive forward-projection can enable me to put the possible incident and 'hot-shot' student (and his behaviour) into perspective. I don't have to take it personally.

Provoking swearing

A teacher walked up to a girl who was slyly doing maths homework in a history lesson. The teacher grabbed the work, said: 'What do you call this? Eh?' and proceeded to tear it up. The girl said, with some vehemence: 'You f——ing bitch!'

The student should have said 'Miss, I don't treat you this way and I prefer it if you do not speak to me like that', but she did not have the assertive skill to state her needs clearly, fairly, non-aggressively and convincingly.

In this sense, the teacher 'deserved' the retort, but the student got the suspension.

Address primary behaviour non-confrontationally. Keep a respectful distance; address the behaviour, not the person.

TEACHER: Dianne, what are you doing?
STUDENT: Nothing! (*pouting, arms folded*)
TEACHER: You're doing maths, but this is a history class. What are you supposed to be doing?

The teacher does not say, 'Don't lie to me! what do you think this is?', the teacher is not crowding the student, the eye-contact is clear. She puts the responsibility back on the student. If the student refuses to acknowledge it, the teacher will redirect (not argue, which would feed the power-seeking goal of the student).

Refer to the rule for swearing. 'You know our rule for ——. Use it.' If the swearing is directed at another student: 'David, that's a put-down, and put-downs hurt!'. Be clear, firm, with controlled emotion. If students argue, avoid arguing back.

STUDENT: But you didn't hear what Nick said. You always take his side!
TEACHER: Maybe I didn't hear what Nick said (*tune-in*), but it's still a put-down. I'll speak to you later.

- Use 'I' statements for personal abuse or 'exit': 'I don't speak like that to you; I don't want you to speak like that to me!' (Realise, though, that it can't actually hurt you.)
- Don't demand apologies there and then. You won't get them and it only feeds the unnecessary power struggle. Aim for apology: 'I'll expect an apology later', but be sure to follow up.

- Always follow up with the student, with senior support. *Never ignore or tolerate verbal abuse.* Be prepared to exit for direct verbal abuse and have an exit support policy in place to be used if a student refuses. Hopefully, this will have been established school-wide.

Children swear for effect, for attention and — from early adolescence on — for power or to hurt. Being aware of the goal can help in how you view and perceive swearing and how to better address it.

Swearing and beliefs

I had been called to an upper primary classroom to 'exit' a student who had been disruptive and unco-operative. The school had a well-established procedure that enabled teachers to call for support when needed. Being new to the school, this was my first time as an 'exit agent'.

I entered the room where children were continuing with activities pretty well as usual. In one corner, an 11-year-old girl was talking loudly about what she wasn't going to do. I approached her quietly and asked her to come with me. As if waiting for an opportunity to vent greater anger, she spun around and said: 'You can go and get f———. I don't have to do what you say!'.

These bitter words were spat out with real venom; her eyes sparked with anger, fists were clenched, body tense and ready to fight.

A few years ago, a string of abuse like this would have caused a quite dramatic emotional reaction in me. I would have felt a surge of blood to my face and my heart pumping harder, maybe a rush of anger. Thoughts going through my head would have been something like 'What right has this brash, aggressive person got to abuse me? I've tried really hard for these kids and look what I get! This child just should not be talking like this'.

My reaction today in this situation is different. *I no longer experience the stressful emotional reaction.* This is not because I've become hardened to such abuse, but rather because I have a very different attitude to events like this.

In such a situation I now see a child who needs help to cope more effectively with a life problem. In seeing the child as having the problem, and my role as the mature adult to help the child behave more appropriately and work out better ways of handling difficulties, I am able to cope with the abuse in a very different way. *I don't take the abuse personally.* I am now able to act rationally and calmly when confronted with such abuse, rather than becoming emotionally distressed and dysfunctional in such situations.

My response to the child who had just abused me?

In a quiet, friendly voice: 'Tania, I can see that you are upset. There is a problem here and it needs to be sorted out. I do not want the teaching and learning in this classroom disrupted. Come with me now, please, and we can sort this problem out'. Tania came.

I am not saying that this scenario is the only possibility. There are situations where children like Tania may still refuse to co-operate. Other actions may need to be taken. However, the important point is that I was able to be and act in a rational, sensitive way; to be calm and reassuring rather than emotional in dealing with this situation. I know that I am much more effective now than I used to be in handling such cases.

Alan

Time-out

The issue of time-out has been explored elsewhere (Rogers 1990); suffice it to say here that to be effective, it needs to be seen as a whole-school approach.

- Time-out should be a consequence, not just a punishment (the short-term consequence of being directed away from the social group).
- Time-out should not be counter-reinforcing.
- The procedure should be explained clearly to all students at the beginning of the year.
- It clearly is necessary for some students to have a 'breather', but it is equally important for the staff and the rest of the class to have a breather, too. 'I'm so angry right now that if I do anything I might just blow, so I'm directing you to leave now' — or 'Since you won't calm down, I have to ask you to leave. I hope we can get together later and work this out, but if you are not willing to settle down, it's better that you leave now' (Glasser 1991,p.140). This provides temporary withdrawal of the stimulation — the attention of the social group. It also shows clearly where the line (that must not be overstepped) is drawn and that safety and treatment rights of teachers and students will be protected.
- Time-out gives a clear message to the total school community about non-negotiable behaviours. We ought not to send students out for chewing gum, not having equipment or calling out, or for uniform misdemeanours, lateness and other low-level issues, easily dealt with, but rather for threats to safety, abuse and *persistent* disruption when the student refuses clear opportunities to own the behaviour.
- Responsibility for follow-up of *any* uses of time-out needs to include the duty-of-care teacher who exited the student.

A supportive time-out policy needs to include options, perhaps a 'cascade model' (from least to most intrusive):

- in-class COT (cool-off-time) for lower and even middle primary (5-minute time-out sitting away from others and timing oneself with an egg-timer, sitting on a bean bag in the corner, remembering that time-out is a consequence — this can be explained as part of the classroom rules);
- a 5-minute (not half-hour) 'cool off to rethink' outside the room (acceptable for some students if the whole-school approach agrees on this form of time-out, leaving the door open: 'Sit down and come in when you are ready to work by the fair rules';
- sending the student to a *nominated* person — either a colleague close by or a senior teacher (preferably not the principal);
- a cue system for dangerous students, or students who refuse to leave when directed;
- a clear record-keeping and follow-up procedure (see Appendix II).

Collegiate exit or supported exit

One successful process for exit is to use an established cue system between peers. We call this the 'exit card' system. Each teacher in the school, unit or building has a small card (generally coloured). It may have 'exit' written on it, and the room number.

The process is planned, with *all staff*, as a viable *intermediate* time-out falling between a 5-minute break outside the room and being sent or taken to the VP.

It is used with students who would tend to do a runner if sent or who refuse to leave, throwing an even greater fit!

- A student from room A will take a postcard-size red card with the room number recorded on it to teacher B. Teacher B receives the card, knowing already what the agreed procedure is, and calmly tells her class that she is going across the corridor (support teachers in such plans need to be spatially close) to get Troy (in room A). Her class frowns and sighs, but they know it's for Troy's good ('Oh, not Troy again!').

- Teacher B appears in teacher A's doorway and takes in the scene immediately: Troy is running around the room in 'gaga' mode. The supporting colleague directs Troy to come with her: 'Troy, come with me now. C'mon'. She speaks firmly and clearly, expecting compliance.

- In severe cases, where the student is totally out of control, a third teacher may be required. In such cases the child needs physical removal from his peers, but this needs to be done with dignity, calmly, with a message of reassurance to the class. 'We're just helping Troy out for a while till he stops being upset (or angry)'.

- The point is that such an exit and subsequent time-out is planned ahead with all concerned. It is normally enough for the exited student to go to a colleague's room to simply cool off for 10 to 15 minutes and then be allowed to go back across the corridor to the home room. At secondary level, it may be necessary to leave the student there until the bell goes, and follow up later. The message given to the exited student is 'When you are ready to work by the fair rules, you can go back to Miss Davie's room'. Sometimes the exit card may need to be sent earlier in the disruptive/acting-out cycle to target the support colleague's help.

It is important that the exited student not be overly reinforced by any discussion or questioning. He or she is there to cool off and settle until ready (or until deemed by the support teacher to be ready) to go back. The student needs no work or special privileges at this time. Some senior staff actually give exited students special jobs, which becomes counter-reinforcing at the time of exit.

If the student does a runner, jumps through a window (hopefully not on the second floor), climbs a tree or plays up significantly in the colleague's room, the card is sent to the office. If leaving a room to support a colleague close by is considered a risk, the card can be used to summon a free teacher (senior or otherwise) via the office.

Developing special behaviour agreements or contracts for behaviour

Students with high frequency, intensity (seriousness) and duration of disruptive behaviour need special discipline-plans alongside normal classroom and school-policy guidelines.

Special plans can be drawn up with the student and the class teacher or co-ordinator, within a whole-school model.

It is important that the school administration and the teaching staff acknowledge how draining such students are: they put more stress on the school than any other handicapping condition (Wragg 1989).

The support needed to address such students requires a whole-school approach and one which gives due support to affected teachers as well as to the disruptive student. Any special plans involving a 1–1 meeting with such students are geared to learning and social success, and will concentrate on present behaviour, attitude and thinking and on future success. Whatever the precipitating causes, and whatever long-term counselling or welfare support may be given, the school will best serve the disaffected student by treating him or her as being able, with support (a plan), to make better, more effective choices that will influence learning and the sense of belonging at this school.

Any contract agreement needs to focus on several things.

'Ownership' by the student

The teacher will listen to the student as well as explain (specifically) the problem behaviour (which may briefly be modelled). The teacher will then enable the student to reformulate and clarify the problem and to look for a workable solution — will enable the student to come up with a plan that is simple and achievable. The teacher does not hastily accept the solutions — in fact, may have to temper promises to be perfect!

Even very young children can own a contract process by two-way dialogue and negotiation. Discuss what the student is doing and how it is affecting others. However, if students show no interest in working with a teacher on a behaviour agreement, there's not much point in forcing it on them. Let them know that they can work with you to learn how to change their behaviour for the better, but that if they choose not to do so, then they will face the consequences of the school policy. Nevertheless, your door is open.

Clear, specific, non-judgmental support

Support the student by developing a collaborative approach to the problem of the behaviour without getting into another counselling session. It is generally a wiser course to have counselling (for disturbed, socioemotional issues) separately from the contracting process.

A contract is not a consequence. It is not a new punishment. While it often includes consequences, it is a process to support the student (and teachers) in improving behaviour and, consequently, self-esteem. It will therefore involve a commitment by the initiating teacher to support the student in some way in keeping to the plan.

Support of the class or subject teacher

Support needs to be given to all subject (or class) teachers who teach a student on such a contract. They need copies of the contract or plan or agreement, an explanation of its philosophy (although the school policy may already have this written in) and suggestions as to how they can encourage, support and even discipline the student 'within the contract' (that is, adopt a non-confrontational approach that concentrates on the behaviour — teachers use simple directions and rule-reminders, and avoid arguments by giving clear choices within the contract and consequences).

Brief and concise contracts

The contract needs to be brief, describing one or two key behaviours to start with and stating in positive terms the responsibilities of each person involved. State the positive as well as any negative consequences in fulfilling the contract or agreement. It is most important that all teachers support students in their efforts to work by the contract.

Change takes time: keep the goals clear and brief, discuss — even rehearse — them with students, and review them so that students can monitor their progress.

Brainstorming effective discipline/management practice

1 What do you (or the group) believe effective discipline practices to be? It is important to be specific rather than to use words or phrases such as 'being firm', 'being strict or tough' or even 'showing respect to the student'. Give examples of how being strict, firm, tough, fair or respectful *sounds* when dealing with a student who is calling out, butting in, avoiding tasks, wandering from seat to seat, challenging the teacher.

2 What sort of rules or classroom agreements have you established with your students? How were they established? How positively are they stated? How fair or just is your opinion? What part did the students have in forming them? Have you discussed rights, responsibilities and consequences with your students?

3 How would you describe your discipline style? Are there areas you need to modify? How will you go about accessing and developing skills you may need?

What do you actually, characteristically, say when you're under pressure to discipline on the spot? Are you aware of the phrases you characteristically use? Does it matter? Do you have a least-to-most intrusive plan about what to say when?

4 How much forward planning have you done in this area of management? Effective discipline and management is marked by a number of factors, not least of which is the ability to consciously control our relational behaviour: what we say, how much we say, when to tactically ignore some things and become angry about others (showing anger, not aggression), how we say things (tone), and how we move into and out of discipline transactions with students.

5 If our aim is to lead, teach, guide, motivate and challenge children towards self-discipline and respect for the rights of others (as well as of themselves), are some practices better or worse relative to that aim? What are *better* practices? What are *good* practices? The moment we use the word '*good*' or even '*better*', we've set up a standard. What is that standard at this school, and in your own classroom or counselling or leadership practice?

Positive discipline and welfare

When in the Elton Report (1989) school atmosphere was discussed, it was noted that negative atmospheres in schools included things like widespread litter and graffiti, teachers starting lessons late and finishing them early, teachers simply ignoring bad behaviour in corridors and playgrounds, pupils regularly skipping lessons and getting away with it, lack of any display of pupils' work and the regular use of inappropriate punishment.

In schools where a supportive ethos is promoted, staff work together with pupils, where feasible, to 'lift the corporate game'. Schools with a negative tone or atmosphere suffer more from disruptive behaviours than those with a positive tone. Even the standards of work and 'life-chances' are improved when schools actively pursue a supportive environment. In such an environment discipline is addressed as a preventative issue, not only as a corrective issue.

Guiding principles

For a school to develop positive discipline, there need to be clear guiding principles agreed on by all staff and reflecting the school's norms or central values. Rutter (1979) notes several studies showing the effects of norms that are more powerful when they are clearly established as applying to a whole social group, and when the group itself is cohesive.

Nowhere is this more important than in the area of discipline, classroom management and student welfare. These guiding principles seek to establish:

- a balance between rights and responsibilities;
- responsible learning and social interaction;
- enhanced esteem and welfare for all members of the school community;
- a stable and secure learning and social environment.

A sense of value and place

Central to all discipline and welfare is the need for staff *and pupils* to feel valued and respected as persons. Of course pupils need discipline, but with a focus that actively treats them with respect and dignity even when a teacher needs to show appropriate anger or initiate appropriate consequences.

Balancing rights and responsibilities

All students need to recognise that due rights (to be safe, feel safe, learn, be treated with respect) are balanced by responsibility and fair rules. This is no less true of teachers, who are primary models of rights-giving behaviours.

It is expected that students will be treated with respect whether in classroom discipline, in the carrying out of consequences, when special contractual arrangements are made or even when punishments and sanctions are applied.

Treating students within a choice-and-consequences framework

Whatever their social background, students will be treated as if they can make appropriate choices relevant to age, development and known rules and consequences. No one is a mere victim and no one should be simply excused responsibility and accountability because he or she is 'disturbed'. For consequences to be useful, they need to be logical, fair, clear and, where possible, known in advance.

One of the central messages of effective discipline is 'behaviour ownership'. It depends on how that discipline is exercised. Students are taught and given choices within the fair rules, and consequences — as distinct from empty threats — are made clear.

Establishing school-wide rules

School rules (including rules for corridors, playgrounds and excursions) will be explained to students and discussed, and at classroom level may be negotiated. Wherever possible, rules ought to be reasonable, fair, clear, enforceable (and enforced when blatantly broken), economical and phrased in a positive way. Ideally, when students as well as staff participate in formulating the rules, there is the possibility that they will be seen as purposeful, logical guidelines for behaviour — mechanisms for protecting individual and group rights rather than arbitrary restrictions on freedom.

Rules should be taught, explained or discussed at the beginning of the year. Classroom rules can be reviewed each term.

At secondary school level, rules will normally be developed at a year or faculty level to establish consistency, and each subject teacher will discuss and 'own' those rules at classroom level with the students.

The consequences of rule-breaking need to be taught and discussed so that students can distinguish between meeting consequences and merely being punished.

Minimising unnecessary confrontation, embarrassment or ridicule

Whether addressing a student who is calling out in class, running in the corridor or arguing with you on playground duty, intentional embarrassment is *unnecessary* and is always counterproductive. Some teachers even believe it is necessary! But children dislike this teacher behaviour more than any other. Respect is an *action*. Effective teachers model, invite and expect respect rather than demand, beg or plead for it.

Avoiding long-winded argumentative approaches or arguments

Again, address the behaviour rather than the secondary issues.

TEACHER: Comic in your bag (in class time) or on my desk, thanks, Paul (*direction with simple choice*)

STUDENT: Wasn't reading it.

TEACHER: Maybe you weren't (*tune-in*) but I want you to put it in your bag and get on with your work, thanks. (See pp. 37, 45, 101 for extension of this skill.)

Generally speaking, secondary issues such as pouting, sulky tones, closed body language are

The difference between consequences and punishment

Consequences Based on:	Punishment Based on:
reality of situation — logical relation to misbehaviour, 'fitting' as much as possible	power and authoritarianism often no relation to act
mutual respect	superior/inferior relationship (sub-ordination)
separation of deed from doer (child is acceptable, behaviour is not)	moral judgment (child is bad)
adult recognition of child's goal, keeping calm (controlled) and withdrawing from provocation	adult being unaware of child's goal, wanting to control child instead of having the child learn internal control
child being presented with a choice and consequence within known, fair rules	child having no choice
child experiencing consequences of own behaviour	child seeing imposition by authority figure
child seeing relevance of consequence and having opportunity to try again	past deeds often held against the child (punishment escalating)

best addressed after class or at another time when there is no audience to feed the student's desire for attention or power.

Actively promoting positive behaviours
Do this by encouragement and with appropriate individual and team rewards (discussed with staff and students alike). There are many ways to enhance the social, personal and welfare aspects of schooling: a strong pastoral-care system through form, house or home-group teachers; elective programs; school excursions and cross-age programs. A school needs to consider carefully the wellbeing (welfare) of its students, as this too has a bearing on how discipline is perceived when it is applied.

Discipline is seen as a purposeful activity that seeks to promote positive behaviour rather than an activity that simply overdwells on negative or 'bad' behaviour. Teachers are therefore encouraged to make discipline plans with the advice and support of colleagues (for classroom and playground behaviours).

Establishing clear exit, time-out and follow-up procedures school-wide
Distinguish between consequences, counselling and contracts as appropriate follow-up to classroom and playground disruptions. Some consequences will be short term, such as sitting away from others and working, if too noisy, or cleaning up spit-balls and other mess after class. Others are applied later in the day — or several days later — and may involve writing out behaviour explanations during detention, doing work around the school (if school property has been damaged) or isolation from social play for a few days (for school bullies). Time-out should be seen as a consequence rather than a chance for counselling. Counselling is often associated with consequences such as time-out but may, especially for 'at-risk' students, be saved for a special counselling time. So, too, should time be set aside for contractual behaviour agreements, when children need to be calm and not to associate the contract-time with consequences or punishment.

Actively encouraging peer support (for staff)

This should be the norm for moral and structural support, problem solving and planning in discipline and management.

No teacher, at whatever level of experience, ought to feel a failure in seeking or asking for support. If we see a staff member struggling or experiencing difficulty with hard-case students or a 'reputation' class, the school ought to provide workable support processes.

While we clearly cannot make a teacher feel supported, we can actively create and encourage a 'culture' of support. Rutter et al. (1979, p.136) make this point.

> It was striking ... in the less successful schools teachers were often left completely alone to plan what to teach, with little guidance or supervision from their ... colleagues and little co-ordination with other teachers to ensure a coherent course from year to year.

We could apply this observation to discipline policy and practice also.

Schools can include in their discipline and welfare policies guidelines for enhancing a peer-support focus — a focus where problems are solved on a team basis rather than by saying 'It's your problem, Jack!'.

Dealing with 'hard-case' students

Students with high frequency and intensity of disruptive behaviour will be dealt with on a team basis. A plan will be worked out involving all relevant parties (parents, care-givers, co-ordinators, students). This plan needs to be:

- simple;
- 'owned' by all the parties;
- referring to the three Rs of the school (rights, responsibilities and fair rules);
- specific, clear and achievable;
- addressing the positive outcomes as well as the negative outcomes;
- supportive in emphasis, not merely punitive.

PART 2

A SUPPORTIVE SCHOOL ENVIRONMENT

Chapter 5

Building a supportive school environment

A supportive school environment exemplifies the way a leadership team sets the tone and quality of a school's life — how its culture and ethos is built. It is achieved by means of an active and deliberative process — it is never accidental. It is a purposeful, collaborative model of decision making that does not deny an active and motivating leadership vision.

Much has been made in the literature these days of a school's 'vision' or 'mission'. Essentially this concerns the way a school's leadership can set its major goals by discussion and shared decision making, and how it develops preferred practices through which to turn the goals into working reality.

It is how a school can build a culture, an ethos that marks that school as a place where all members of its community have an opportunity to balance rights and responsibilities as learners, leaders, parents, guides, mentors or colleagues.

While all schools have had 'mottoes' — have theoretically striven for excellence, that elusive goal is only realised in any shape or form when a school sets out to determine what it really wants and how it intends to get it.

Two schools: different in looks, in culture, in outcomes

Visiting several schools in a 'low socioeconomic area' I noticed, yet again, how powerful an impression an individual school can make.

School A
The fence is bashed and graffiti-ridden; it has been like that for ages. The school sign is damaged (again) and half the letters are missing. No welcome to this school. What trees, shrubs and flower beds there are look wan and disconsolate. There is a lot of old rubbish banked up under the bushes and shrubs.

The entrance is darkish wood, cavenous, unwelcoming. A few oldish chairs, a little artwork, a notice board, a folded picture of HM the Queen (wrinkled where the water got in). The staff room was dour, not the cleanest, and with not a pot plant in sight.

School B
This school is in the same area. As you approach you see a sign, obviously new (I found out that it was the third sign in the space of fifteen months — 'It's worth it', said the principal. 'The fence was the first thing we worked on, and then the shrubs and flowerpots round the entrance.')

As you approach the front entrance (clearly signed in several languages), there is a long, brick flowerbox with a host of flowers spilling over. 'We asked the local TAFE (Technical and Further Education) college if their bricklaying students would like a project! They were pleased to work with us.' I noticed, too, the ample rubbish bins and seats, most near shade trees.

The entrance was a clear feature: there was attractive seating and the toilets, unfortunately near the foyer, had been attractively screened off to give staff a bit of privacy. 'Only cost $20.00 for the timber trellis and a few creeping-ivy pot-plants.'

The paintwork was light, there were nice curtains to the glass-enclosed office. A coffee table near the comfortable seats contained several photo albums of recent school events, activities and programs. On one wall a display showed *all* members of staff (including cleaners, typists and other ancillary staff) and photos of all classes.

The artwork was beautifully displayed (some on easels, as a feature) and class projects adorned each corridor. It presented itself as a school that cared for and applauded the efforts of its students.

I asked the principal if there ever was graffiti or damage. 'Oh, sure, but we clean it off as soon as possible. We've got a very supportive cleaning staff and we installed outside lights as well.

'We started by asking students, staff and, later, parents how we could make our school a better place to be in. Most of the suggestions came by this collaborative approach.'

- Each class has a role in caring for a section of the ground, looking after trees, shrubs, and so on. 'We give time for this within the week's activities.
- 'We inform parents regularly of our successes and needs and problems, and they've shown great support.
- 'Each class (with its teacher) has sent home a copy of the class rules and responsibilities, drawn up with the students. This reflects our whole-school rights and responsibilities approach.
- 'We also ring up parents when particularly difficult students have behaved well and shown responsibility and co-operation (that caused some interest the first time we rang up with positive comments!).' On any major issue in the school, each teacher is encouraged to conduct a classroom meeting to gather facts, explore solutions and choose a workable action plan to involve necessary personnel.

Although the example I've quoted is a primary school in the western suburbs of Melbourne, the same is true of any effective secondary school. Something can always be done, and although the things may seem small — pot-plants in the staff room, a rostered 'tea-person' and special morning teas (perhaps better tea-bags), signs, displays of work, special afternoon teas, cross-age tutoring, a *class* afternoon tea — they have a significant overall effect on school tone, especially for visitors and parents but mostly for those who have to work there.

Environment for teachers

This is true, too, for staff. Even laying a bit of carpet, installing some better furniture and a few pot-plants, retimetabling classes with difficult students to share the load and staggering bell-times to reduce traffic flow in the corridors — these things can have a significant effect. Again ask staff for suggestions.

- Clarify the current situation; get the data.
- Look at alternatives; discuss them (in small, mixed-teacher groups).
- Choose workable and feasible solutions.
- Set up an action plan (who, when, where and how?).

While this may sound basic, commonsense, I've been in many schools where the environment shows little trace of care for teacher or student alike. Yet there is always something that can be done, provided that we look for solutions together.

To most people it is axiomatic that environment influences behaviour. Building positive working environments in our schools should rank among the highest priorities.

Schools have begun to realise that relying on punishment and imposed authority means fighting a seemingly endless but losing battle with students. However, adopting a whole-school positive discipline policy — and, by implication, similar individual classroom policies — can break this course, and thereby behavioural problems and consequent teacher stress can be reduced.

The potential benefits of using the whole-school process are:
- a positive, preventative approach to discipline;
- enhanced interstaff support networks;
- staff development in interpersonal communication skills, including active listening, negotiation, conflict resolution, problem solving and assertiveness;
- involvement of parents and students;
- a better understanding on the part of teachers, students and parents of why the school has certain rules and policies;
- a staff secure in the knowledge that when problems arise, definite procedures are in place that will support them — thus there are many fewer 'crises'.

Positive Discipline 1990

In short, a positive discipline policy is an attempt to state, as unambiguously as possible, how the school will seek to teach, guide, encourage, lead and motivate students to behave responsibly, to 'own' the choices inevitable in social behaviour and to respect the rights of all members of the school community.

Ten characteristics of an effective school
1 Commitment to commonly identified norms and goals.
2 Collaborative planning, shared decision-making and collegial work in a framework of experimentation and evaluation.
3 Positive leadership in initiating and maintaining improvement.
4 Staff stability.
5 Continuing staff development linked to the school's pedagogical and organisational needs.
6 Carefully planned and co-ordinated curriculum, catering for the needs of all students.
7 High level of parental involvement and support.
8 The pursuit and recognition of school-wide values rather than individual values.
9 Maximum use of learning time.
10 The active and substantial support of the responsible education authority.

Lowe & Istance (1989)

A whole school approach at work
One school using this approach spelled out this process in five key areas:
- classroom management and teaching strategies;
- parent involvement;
- discipline procedures;
- professional development and staff welfare; and
- appropriate curriculum.

A subcommittee worked on each of these issues. A key group (or working party) reported the focus of these issues back to parents, students and staff. It took some time, during which teachers, parents and students had the opportunity to examine attitudes and practices relevant to positive discipline, management and welfare.

The overall goal was positive teacher–student relationships and the development of practices that would enhance that goal in teaching, learning and social areas:
- work requirements are spelled out at the start of each semester;
- assignment and reporting techniques to be used are fully explained;
- lesson preparation is adequate and assists in class control;
- relevant curriculum, appropriate to the level of the student, is delivered in a suitable way;

- behavioural expectations in each teacher's class are discussed with the class at regular intervals to make the students *aware* of expectations and, particularly, of consequences;
- professional development of staff [is encouraged] in all aspects of teaching and learning, positive discipline skills and management skills;
- peer support of one's own colleagues [is given].

The discipline–management process involved each teacher having a discipline plan with several common elements: clear, fair, 'owned' rules; known consequences; a skills-based approach to the corrective language of discipline; a least-to-most intervention approach and clear follow-up.

Where the aforementioned criteria are being met in the classrooms, the students:

1 are aware of teacher expectations in each subject area;
2 are aware of the consequences of possible actions *before* they do something wrong;
3 are aware that there are steps to be followed in the classroom-management process;
4 are aware that good and proper behaviour is acknowledged before poor behaviour is corrected;
5 are aware that where poor behaviour is corrected, it will be accompanied by a reminder of the consequences of repeated poor behaviour for that class.

This co-operative model is seen as more effective and therefore the time-out room no longer fitted into this process. It was felt that flexibility in discipline strategies and less regimentation in class management was more positive in terms of teacher–student relationship.

The school also included a school-wide demerit system that stresses the provision of a safe, attractive environment where students and staff work and behave in a co-operative manner towards one another. Unlike some demerit systems, it also provides a framework for responsible behaviour in that the student is encouraged to accept responsibility for his or her behaviour and then to co-operate with staff members (and relevant support staff) to avoid any punitive measures; for example, in order to get five demerits, the student must have consciously *chosen* not to co-operate on at least five occasions.

'We also have a student management committee comprising parents, students and teachers — they make recommendations directly to school council regarding policy in discipline, management and student welfare. In 1990, the first full year of this positive discipline approach, there were less than 800 demerits, less than one demerit per student for the year — a fair testimony to the co-operative model of student management. When we operated detentions in 1988 we had *thousands* of them to process in the course of the year!'

Tom

Benefits of a whole-school approach

In a pilot study on the benefits of a whole-school approach to the management of student behaviour, Peter Hamilton (1986) indicated that:

> Teachers in pilot schools showed *lower levels of stress* as measured by a Teacher Occupational Stress Questionnaire compared with teachers in control schools, especially on the factor working with students.

My own observations are that when teachers work together to assess what is happening in confrontations with students, what sorts of things we as teachers believe and do to address conflict and how effectively current strategies meet our goals (of reasonable coping and student ownership of behaviour), then they feel better. They know they are working from a common understanding, addressing common issues and sharing common skills, practices and approaches. Uncertainty is also reduced, because set/agreed procedures are in place across the school.

Teachers in pilot schools *rated their experience of students' misbehaviour as lower* than those teachers in control schools.

This is often due to a common, skilled approach school-wide to managing pupil disruption. Teachers also attributed disruptive behaviour to factors within the school environment rather than merely to factors outside the school's control. As Rutter et al. (1979) have shown, a school can significantly affect the social-interactive and educational-academic results of its students in significant ways regardless of socioeconomic status. When schools identify the factors under their control in relation to the way they discipline (lead, guide, teach, manage towards self-control) and educate generally, then changes can be made — the key area being, of course, the manner in which students, teachers and parents relate and co-operate with one another.

Central to this notion is the existence of fundamental expertise *within* the school; it then needs only opportunity, a focus and a process to bring about a whole-school approach by utilising that expertise.

Hamilton (1986) also noted that:

> pilot schools developed a clear expression of norm, aims and practices in a school discipline policy, along with diminishing rates of suspensions, corporal punishment (now abolished), referrals to senior management.

It has been my experience that the results are the same when a school:
- analyses what is happening, commonly, in discipline/management;
- surveys staff, parents and students;
- allows healthy discussion and debate about principles and practices of reasonable discipline (what *values* do we put on different kinds of discipline?);
- analyses what it is trying to achieve in student discipline and management (the goals);
- identifies the skills that will better address those goals;
- encourages in-service of staff in alternative approaches to, say, punitive styles;
- expresses this in a coherent and clear way as school policy.

As noted by Wilson and Corcoran (1988, p.86), the primary characteristics of an 'ideal' work environment include:

1 shared goals and high expectations to create strong communal identity;
2 respectful and dignified treatment as professionals by superiors and by parents and students;
3 participation by teachers in the decisions affecting their work;
4 regular opportunities for interaction and sharing with colleagues that promote a collective identity;
5 recognition and rewards for effort and achievement;
6 opportunities for professional growth;
7 decent working conditions.

The report *Teacher Stress in Victoria* (1989) noted that 'an absence of shared beliefs (or culture) within the school about fit and proper student and teacher behaviour' and 'differences underlying views about discipline practices in the same school' contributed to teacher stress.

Fig. 5.1 School policy (discipline and management)

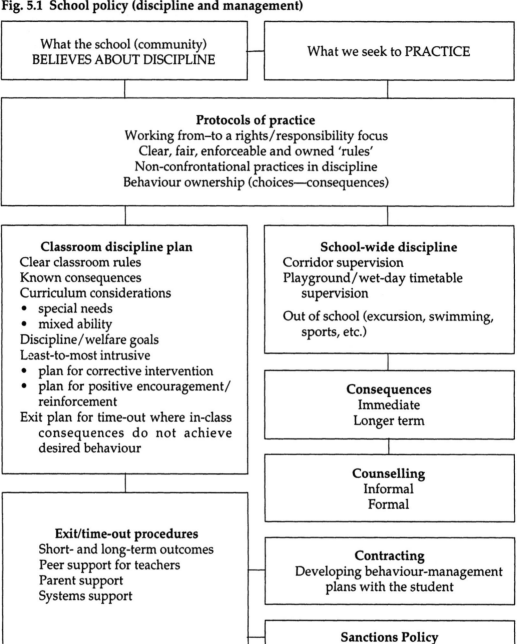

One of the suggestions in the report was:

That each school be required to have a published discipline policy (developed in consultation with parents, students and staff) and to develop mechanisms to ensure that it is understood and applied consistently within the school (pp. 34, 35).

A school discipline policy

One of the aims of a school-wide approach to discipline, management and welfare is the expression of beliefs and preferred practices in a policy. Since the abolition of corporal punishment, many Australian schools have pursued a policy approach to school-wide discipline and behaviour management. In some states the emphasis has been to use alternative terms instead of the word 'discipline' — for instance, student behaviour-management, student welfare, positive discipline, developing responsibility, supportive school environment. As noted earlier, effective schools are supportive schools that allow 'ownership, with leadership, in policy development.

The Elton Report (1989) identifies several areas of school management essential for effective and positive maintenance of school discipline:

- fostering a sense of community;
- taking a lead in setting aims and standards;
- establishing and maintaining workable internal and external communication systems;
- encouraging collective responsibility;
- giving effective support to their staffs;
- the directing of the curriculum and organisational planning;
- the management of staff by a consultative and appropriately collaborative style.

Leadership

I've asked countless teachers who whinge about their leaders: 'Well, what do you want from your principal or vice-principal?' Here are some answers:

- someone who'll support you — back you up when needed;
- someone who will listen to your side of a story (if you're late, or haven't got a report in on time, or a parent complains);
- but someone who still knows when to be firm;
- someone who will get things done when asked (mending a broken light, remedying lack of equipment);
- someone who lets you know and encourages you when you've done a good job.

Most of all they seem to want someone who gives them the feeling and belief that they are valued, respected and listened to as people as well as professionals. As one teacher said to me: 'The best support is to be valued'.

They don't want much from their leaders!

> A boss drives. A leader leads.
> A boss relies on authority. A leader relies on co-operation.
> A boss says 'I'. A leader says 'We'.
> A boss creates fear. A leader creates confidence.
> A boss knows how. A leader shows how.
> A boss creates resentment. A leader breeds enthusiasm.
> A boss fixes blame. A leader fixes mistakes.
> A boss makes work drudgery. A leader makes work interesting.
>
> Glasser, 1991, p. 1

In creating a policy process, the school ought to consider various courses of action.

Be collaborative in nature. Involve staff and (wherever possible) students and parents — rather than have the policy dictated as a fait accompli by the principal.

Allow a process of values clarification about discipline, punishment, rights, responsibilities, rules, sanctions and roles in discipline procedures. Teachers, students and parents often have different levels of understanding and perception about what these aspects of discipline mean. To some, discipline means merely punishment, to others self-discipline, to still others control, conformity or 'obedience' to teachers. Unless there is reasonable discussion and agreement on the philosophy of discipline and student management, the school will see little success in the actual day-to-day practices. What we believe is reflected in how we act; the school policy is revealed in room 17, not merely on a piece of paper.

Allow time for surveying, gaining data and feedback and communicating the outcomes back to affected parties. Although this is time-consuming, it gives 'ownership' to the process, especially when reviewing school rules and consequences (see the survey in appendix I). Among other things, a school discipline policy outlines what rules are fair, reasonable and necessary to promote safety, learning and harmony in social relationships. One of the key outcomes of a positive discipline policy is to enhance and cultivate self-discipline in the upholding of the rules.

Allow time during the review process to raise awareness of alternative approaches. Time should be taken to study examples of other approaches to discipline in the literature and in successful practices — see, for example, C.M. Charles, *Building Classroom Discipline: From Models to Practice.*

Run a series of workshops on various discipline/management approaches. Invite credible practitioners to share with staff, explore the tough questions and even role-play effective non-confrontational but assertive strategies. These role-plays(with two or three teachers) need to be carefully structured, planned, even scripted, to allow definable skills to be seen and tried (see for example 'Gentle Assertive Role Plays' in Rogers (1990).

Discuss suggested classroom practices that better reflect the school's aims for discipline and management (see chapter 4).
1　Have clear, fair, 'owned' rules to protect all rights of all persons in the room.
2　Have a non-confrontational style based on assertion rather than aggression.
3　Plan a verbal repertoire that is brief, minimises argument or procrastination, addresses behaviour and implies the choice given to students to own their behaviour. Staff can even write up (or down!) examples of how they.can verbally (most discipline is verbal) address common discipline issues such as calling out, time-wasting, task-avoidance and fighting over property.

Many of the schools I've worked in actually have a suggested classroom plan for staff to adopt (see appendix I).

Outline the roles of support personnel and how they interact with that of the classroom teacher. The policy needs to set out the respective roles of staff from year-level co-ordinator, pastoral-care or home-room teacher, form tutor and counsellor up to deputy principal and principal.

How do these roles operate and support one another in discipline and management? Are there specific referral responsibilities? If so, what are the limits of that referral?

Plan follow-up procedures to be observed by class and subject teachers. Where the subject or class teacher has a commitment to and interest in the welfare of a student he or she has exited from the classroom, then the outcome is generally more effective. If the matter is merely passed on to a senior teacher, the actual problem (existing between the class teacher and the student) is not effectively addressed.

A number of schools I have worked with have a process that recognises two significant points concerning this issue.
1　The exit of a student is treated as a significant disciplinary measure. No teacher should be labelled a failure for needing to exit significantly disruptive students where breaches of safety, aggression, violence or persistent disruption occur.
2　However, upon short-term referral to a colleague (senior teacher or otherwise), it is expected that the teacher who initiated the exit will, within the same week, meet with the student to work out a plan for consequences, counselling and/or 'contracting' for future successful outcomes in class. If the teacher needs a third party to help in the conflict-resolution process, it is expected that a senior staff member will make a time to meet with both initiating teacher and student to resolve the problem in some way. Ultimately, the student has to go back to the teacher, anyway, which is why (when the heat has gone down) that initiating teacher needs to be involved.

Ensure that policy procedures are consistent. It is essential to be consistent in the use of consequences — are they logical, fair, fitting? Generally speaking, it is better to list consequences for major issues rather than to include every contingency. What is important to stress is that consequences be:

- fair and reasonable (it is the certainty of the consequence rather than the severity that is important);
- related to the disruptive behaviour (rather than unrelated detention, such as copying from a dictionary, copying the rules, writing lines);
- applied consistently and with respect when the heat has gone down.

If I tell a student to stay back and clean up the clay balls he was flicking around in art — fine! If I add vilification: 'You're stupid — what are you? Now you can just clean the whole clay area for that', desire for 'getting-back' destroys the related, reasonable nature of the consequence chain.

Other areas in which consistency is important are:

- exit from the classroom in the short term, and time-out practices (see appendix II);
- corridor and wet-day duty;
- playground discipline;
- excursion discipline practices;
- use of counselling and contracting approaches within the school policy practices;
- sanctions such as in-school or out-of-school suspension and withdrawals (from group play, excursions, swimming and so on).

Wet-day timetabling

We worked on a wet-day timetable, using a collaborative model.

- We discussed current procedures and practices from all angles.
- We wanted a fair policy outcome that included senior staff doing duty of care as well.
- We discussed it with children.
- Suggestions for games and activities were made (rostered rooms for many activities and other rooms for board games and electives, rather than just each grade using its own room).
- The library and art rooms were rostered.
- We drew up a timetable to allocate activities and roster all teachers. The value of having senior staff (even the principal) on a roster is that the children get to see them as other than discipline figures.

Arthur

Publishing the policy

It is useful to have a committee or working party to integrate the review process. At each stage the working party will feed back to staff (even to parents and students) the outcomes of the review. Draft guidelines can then be published, following feedback processes. No policy document is published in one operation; the key is to facilitate the process of review, discussion, workshops on preferred approaches, implementation and review. It may take twelve months or more to get a policy document to its final form, and even that needs to be reviewed every five years, as with any policy document. Students can contribute to the publishing process by writing and illustrating or by producing a summary version at classroom level — this is particularly effective in primary school settings.

The document needs to address the fundamentals noted earlier (essentially beliefs and practices) with adequate brevity — not an easy task!

- How old is the policy?
- When was it last renewed?
- Is it written down or merely an idea in someone's head?
- Who wrote it?
- Were parents or students involved in any way?
- Does the policy define what this school means by discipline?
- What are the goals of discipline? What do we discipline for?
- Are any guiding principles of discipline outlined?
- What are the preferred, stated *practices* of discipline at classroom, corridor, playground and excursion levels?
- Is there a set exit and follow-up procedure for significantly disruptive students?
- When are parents notified?
- What are the roles of support staff and senior staff in discipline/welfare?
- Does the policy outline school rules and classroom rules?
- Does the policy address the longer term discipline issues such as how and what consequences are used? Does it include pastoral-care considerations, the use of counselling and referral procedures, Ministry of Education regulations that may be relevant?
- Does everyone (including parents) have a copy?
- How are staff, especially new staff, in-serviced in the policy?
- Have parents been invited to a workshop on the policy and how it works?

Making the policy work

It is also important at the beginning of a year to in-service staff — especially new staff and first-year teachers — in the school's discipline policy. Each teacher should, of course, have a copy.

The whole point in having a discipline policy (or any policy) is to gain some congruence between preferred (desired) and actual practices:

- to balance preventative, corrective and supportive features of discipline and management (supportive for staff as well as students);
- to enhance the welfare (wellbeing) of students and teachers alike through structural processes (such as rule-making, step-wise approaches to corrective discipline and clear conflict-resolution processes) and through pastoral care on the wider level.

A whole-school approach can do that. It won't be perfect, but it will be the balance that operates in most areas of rational living — a balance of rights and responsibilities with fair rules and fair treatment.

At the end of the day, any discipline program or policy is only as good as (and dependent on):

- the support given by those (our peers) who have to carry it out;
- agreed protocols of practice (our values are communicated this way more than any other);

- the determined application of any skills we possess;
- the essential humanity that is the bottom line in effecting any change for the better and without which even the slickest program would be merely 'paper-policy'.

Whether in a family or in a school, 'systems' essentially consist of persons relating to persons. Some working rights and understanding of mutual responsibility — with some expression in agreed conventions of living and working together ('rules') — are necessary. And if we score eight out of ten in the way we carry out our aims, our intentions, our practices, then there ought to be enough forgiveness and understanding of our fallibility to say: 'Well done! Hang in there'.

> The way in which a school is run can be changed. We know that this is not easy. Changing the nature of an institution can be a long, complicated and uncomfortable process. We recognise that the difficulties involved in breaking into the vicious circle of ineffective performance and low morale can be very great, and that some schools may need a great deal of help in achieving this breakthrough. We are convinced, however, from what we have seen in schools, from research evidence, and from experiences described to us in other countries that successful change can be achieved. The *first* and most important requirement is a positive commitment to change by the headteacher and other senior staff. The *second* is for them to carry as many of the rest of the staff as possible with them and to be open to their suggestions. To see the need for change, heads and teachers need to recognise the school's present atmosphere, particularly from the pupils' point of view. This is not always easy for an insider. *They need to recognise their power to create a different atmosphere, and to be convinced that the changes they make will produce positive responses from the pupils. They then need to work out what practical steps they intend to take and how they are to be taken* [author's italics]. For most schools, effective action starts with the recognition that behaviour problems cannot simply be attributed to factors outside the institution, such as pupils' home backgrounds.
>
> Heads should keep up to date with the research evidence on school effectiveness. This evidence currently suggests:
>
> (a) that school processes and the atmosphere which they produce can have a substantial influence on pupils' behaviour;
>
> (b) that in schools where standards of behaviour are considered unsatisfactory by staff, significant improvements can be achieved through institutional change; and
>
> (c) that perhaps the most important characteristic of schools with a positive atmosphere is that pupils, teachers and other staff feel that they are known and valued members of the school community.
>
> Elton Report (1989)

▼ Chapter 6

Supporting teachers in managing significantly disruptive students

The 1–5 per cent

Most students will evidence some disruptive behaviours at some point in school life. In any school, however, there is a group — figures vary from 1 per cent to 5 per cent (Wragg 1989; Morgan & Jensen 1988) — whose disruptive behaviour, in its degree of frequency, intensity and duration, imposes significant strain on the social, safety and learning rights of others.

Such students are often described as having:
- a social/emotional deficit;
- a significant lack of social skill;
- an intensity of disruptive behaviour stable over time and place (not just in one or two subject areas).

They 'fiddle constantly', are 'motorially restless', have limited attention span, are 'too overactive', 'impulsive', 'aggressive', 'hostile' — all these descriptions are regularly heard and seen in these students' behaviour profiles.

In assessing such students in mainstream settings, a whole-school approach for behaviour disorders would present them as exhibiting behaviour which is:
- persistent in its deviation from the 'norm' (shows a high frequency);
- is severe or intense in its degree of disruption;
- appears to be resistant to conventional attempts to change;
- has been so assessed by a team approach.

Most school referrals spring from this group — they take up a lot of staff time (from class teacher through to visiting psychologist) and emotional effort (inspiring individual and corporate guilt in some), and can hamper the social and learning rights of their peers — not to mention the stress caused to teachers.

Yet these students have a right to an education; in a whole-school approach, this right needs to be balanced against the rights of the teachers and other students. It is my contention that in economically rationalist times, when schools are receiving minimal support for working with such students, we need a whole-school approach. Often the teacher's welfare is the last consideration when servicing the needs of such students. While most teachers would applaud the social-justice aims behind integration, there are many whose classroom-related stress springs from a lack of cohesive support for the school-wide management of such students.

People outside the teaching profession have little idea of how draining the behaviour effect of such students is. Principals too sometimes forget how difficult these students are to manage, and it is often the case that teachers get little formal support (from integration or support teachers). If a school has several such students (most have up to 5 per cent), their management needs to become a school issue rather than merely be left to the unfortunate teacher who scored Dean or Wayne (they're mostly boys) or Tracey!

A whole-school approach emphasises that the school can, and often does, have a significant contribution to make to how disruptive behaviour is dealt with generally, and 'problem' students specifically. In reality, both the student's 'causative pathology' and the school's ecology contribute to any success likely to occur in the child's schooling experience.

Integration

A whole-school approach endorses a primary value that 'behaviourally disordered students' (Morgan & Jensen 1988) should be integrated into mainstream settings wherever and whenever possible. This is the more acute in economically rationalist times, when support services are being drastically reduced. It is clearly unrealistic (and impractical) to send large numbers of disruptive students to outside agencies (or 'experts') for 'quick-fix' or removal. The research on SIN-BIN approaches to significantly or persistently disruptive students demonstrates limited success, and that often only at the off-site centre. Without an emphasis on re-integration into mainstream schooling, exclusion models provide limited opportunity for students to relate socially and educationally in a 'normal' setting.

Peer support

Any approaches that address the problem of conduct disorder, attention-deficit disorder, severe social emotional disturbance or emotional and behavioural disturbance are most effectively carried out on a peer-support basis. *Once teachers recognise terms like these in a behavioural profile they ought to expect wide support, from classroom exit and time-out procedures through to conferencing, behavioural contracts and special programs.*

Any effective influence with such students relies on a change in the working relationships — both short term and long term — of the subject teachers, pastoral teachers and form teachers *working as a team*. When looking at workable options on academic programs and behaviour-change support (for students), it is mandatory that no subject (or class) teacher be left to cope alone. The normal practice is to explore solutions as peers, supporting student and teacher (and often parents) alike.

Finding the solution

Quick-fix solutions are often not possible with such students (they've already got a substantial history of learned behaviours behind them!). These students need time and practical assistance to achieve any classroom success that might reorient their social behaviour to a rights/responsibility/behaviour ownership focus. One excellent resource for school-based programs with such students is Wragg, *Talk Sense to Yourself: A Program for Children and Adolescents.*

Developing a team approach

Initiate and develop, within the school, a *reference group* who have skills in working with such students specifically and in discipline, counselling and behavioural management generally. It will effectively rationalise time spent on such students, but it will be necessary to build in some time-release for the group's effective function. It would be also useful to allow some targeted professional development for such a group. Its members, naturally, will also need street-credibility among the staff.

The reference group can assist teachers to rationalise the best use of school time with such students, and can also (because of its skills):

- assist in the training of teachers in effective management, discipline and follow-up skills;
- act as a referral group for discussion of how to set-up more effective behavioural contracts or programs emphasising self-control and self-management skills for the targeted students (who need to *learn* these skills and receive rehearsal, training and support from teachers to utilise them in mainstream settings);
- set up effective time-out regimes that will (of necessity) involve other teachers;
- enable teachers to set up a system of 'crisis management' for children who display hostile, aggressive or unusually deviant behaviours.

That is, such a group would act both as a *support group* for dealing with such students school-wide (as well as in playground situations) and as a *steering committee* for professional development and policy development on discipline and welfare.

In the function of policy review, members on the steering committee can be co-opted to survey staff and set up professional development workshops (for example, mini-workshops), especially during staff-meeting times. One of the admirable uses of mini-workshops is to encourage staff who are carrying out effective discipline/management practices to share their skills and answer questions about running classroom meetings with students to solve class-related problems.

Making a plan

1   After wide assessment, any plan will need to fit in with the school-wide aims for discipline. At the classroom level it is important that such students not be treated with any radical difference in regard to the balance of rights, responsibilities (especially logical consequences) and the fair rules. The guiding principles (chapter 4) are as relevant for socioemotional, conduct-disordered or attention-deficit-disordered students as for any others. These students need clear, firm, fair, *consistent* treatment, planned ahead of time with the 'extra support'. The aim, though, is the same. How can we enable (not make) Jason to take responsibility for his behaviour? What a plan will do for such students is to assist them (and their teachers and parents) to manage their own behaviour (social and learning) more successfully.

2   It will be necessary to assess the current learning program for such students. There is often a correlation between social behaviour and 'academic' work..

Any learning program contemplated will need to take account of mixed-ability teaching in the setting where the disadvantaged student receives instruction that incorporates:
- individual work-contracts;
- mastery learning;
- balance of co-operative approaches and individual class work where possible;
- peer tutoring, cross-age tutoring;
- balance of non-academic areas of the school's curriculum to build in self-esteem outcomes.
  The key is to decide as a team, to use collegiate planning.
- Set and communicate clear learning goals.
- Sequence units of work with clear explanations and with opportunities for students to give and receive feedback.
- Check students' understanding by rehearsal and questioning approaches.
- Give students ample setting and opportunity to practice the new skills.
- Monitor progress, and give ample and supportive feedback.

3   Clarify the balance of necessary short-term time-out with longer term support through counselling and behavioural contracts (Wragg 1989; Rogers 1990, 1991b).

Students need to know clearly what unacceptable, rights-infringing behaviours are (the non-negotiables of threats to safety, and of aggression or violence); we also need to consider persistent, unremitting disruptive behaviour such as howling, barking, running on tables — 'if he's quiet under the table, tactically ignore him'.

Students need to know clearly what time-out means for them (this is true, of course, for all students). If they (continue to) make it difficult for people to be safe, to feel safe or to learn, they will be asked to:
(a) work away from others;
(b) sit away from others (a cool-off time);
(c) leave the room until they agree to work by the fair rules.

Teachers will need a backup plan to impose time-out on students who refuse to leave, kick the walls, run noisily, climb, or jump through windows. Such a backup plan needs swift application, with no imputation of failure to the initiating teacher. Remember, any plan is as much for teacher (and other student) support as for the disruptive student.

Long-term decisions about balancing appropriate counselling (especially for at-risk students) and behavioural contracting are decided by collegiate planning (Rogers 1991b).

4   Where students require an off-campus (even residential) placement, the emphasis again ought to be on re-integration into a mainstream setting. It is suggested that the student (where feasible) remain on the roll of the host school and the support school as

part-placement back into the school (for instance, with one day a week wholly involved in the off-campus program).

5   In off-campus settings mixed-ability teaching is employed and work-required assessment is used in a program emphasising self-esteem and social-skills development in the context of respectful yet appropriately assertive discipline. Where a student has enjoyed and benefited from such an approach, it is important that on re-entering the host school a contractual approach, involving all teachers working with the student, is entered into.

If re-integration is going to be successful, it cannot afford abrogation simply because of inadequate communication processes.

Joint plans involving all teachers who have a particular student ought to be the norm. They can be set up either by contract arrangement (expressed in some written way) or by clear verbal acknowledgment of how to deal with these students. The philosophy and preferred practices need to be made clear to all. Of course, a subject or class teacher's basic discipline and management may need review if it is not in concert with the school aims for discipline and classroom management.

'Cracking the hard class'

Some classes have a 'reputation' in the school, and these 'hard classes' are not always given to the most confident or competent teachers — a practice that says much about some approaches to teacher welfare. Some schools timetable such classes directly to the latest arrival, or to a first-year teacher.

Where co-ordinators clearly perceive the hard-class issue exists, they need to do a number of things.

*   Set up support structures for the teachers concerned.
*   Plan ahead, getting data from all subject teachers prior to meeting.
    - Who are the problem students, in the main?
    - Is their behaviour consistently problematic across subject areas? If so, where?
    - What behaviours specifically do subject teachers complain of?
    - Can they note how (and what) strategies they've tried in managing the hard-class scenario? Have there been any successes? What are they?

- Call a meeting with all subject teachers of (for example) 8D, to discuss the problem and look for solutions.
- Recognise that it is natural that there will be frustration — even anger — expressed at this meeting, so it is important that the year-level co-ordinator or vice-principal plan it well.
- Find out how the curriculum can be dealt with in relation to these students. Does it really cater for mixed ability? Does it address any of their needs? I've worked with a number of teachers who have used quite creative curriculum solutions to motivate learning and build self-esteem.
- Employ the action-planning approach (see below).
- Use a peer-assisted approach by having a classroom meeting with the hard class, chaired by two members of staff who both teach the class.
  - Establish clear rules for the meeting (speak one at a time, stay on topic, give no put-downs).
  - Seat students in a circle or a half-circle.
  - Alternatively, use the two, four, six method: send off students in pairs for 10 minutes each to be joined by another pair after 10 minutes and then to make groups of six.
  - Ask three basic questions: (a) What is working well in the class? (b) What is not working well in the class? Why? (c) Which areas can we change?
- Use a classroom-meeting format to redirect the group to their rights and responsibilities, rules and consequences.
- Plan the meeting in advance with your colleague. Plan what you hope to achieve at the meeting, and how you will conduct, manage, record suggestions and conclude it.
- Hold mini-meetings in which one colleague takes the class while the other withdraws two or three students at a time to clarify your concern with them: why they think the problem exists and what they intend to do to change their behaviour so that students can work effectively and behave appropriately.
- Consider using 'group reinforcement'. Split the class into mixed-ability groupings; get the class to elect four team leaders by secret ballot and have them sit in groups (choose group names if it's a Year 7 or 8). Use a points system on a weekly score chart. Groups can earn rewards: free-time activities or edible rewards, based on points earned by all four teams (see Rogers 1990, chapter 7).
- Consider splitting a reputation class across several groups.

The key to cracking a hard class is to encourage individual teachers to take a team approach to problem solving.

Developing an action plan

1 What is the problem as you see it (as an individual teacher and/or as a team)? Clarify the issue — get the facts clear by means of a survey or a class or group meeting; check with all parties. If students are involved, give them a chance to tell their side of the story. What you're trying to do is balance mutual considerations and needs with responsibilities.

   Make sure the 'shape' of the problem or issue is as clear as you can make it.

2 Generate possible solutions.

3 Evaluate a feasible, necessary, required solution — one that you believe can best meet your needs at present and can best address the problem.

4 Decide how best the solutions can be implemented; express it in a simple action plan, outlining tasks, support, timeline.

5 Make a time to assess and review how it's going. Most plans need fine-tuning.

This basic approach is relevant for working with all parties in the school community.

Organisational change to support welfare/discipline at the whole-school level

Last year our school had 'one of those' grades. It was a Grade 5 and heavily gender-imbalanced, having seventeen boys to five girls. The girls in the group were 'swamped'. More than half of the boys were regarded as 'behaviour problems'. Two of the grade's students were integration students.

'What will they be like as a Grade 6?' was the question on everyone's lips as their Grade 5 year drew to a close.

Gender imbalance was clearly a problem.

The girls were an almost *unheard* minority.

These students had travelled through the primary school in the same social group. One of these typically 'hard' or 'reputation' classes.

Perhaps it was time for a change?

Other grades in the school also pointed to a need for some kind of restructure. Grade 4 was small — fifteen girls and five boys. A 'good' grade, exactly the opposite of Grade 5. There was a small Grade 3 — fourteen children — and a small group of fifteen Preps.

To spread the load more evenly over the teaching staff, to avoid having the newly appointed VP bound to a grade and to balance the genders in the upper grades while separating the 'behaviour problems' of Grade 5, it was decided to restructure the entire school into multi-age groups. This involved a great deal of discussion and meetings of the whole school community, which was very supportive of the idea. Parents were happy to have some of the social groups rearranged.

This year we have two gender-balanced Grades 5–6, a 3–4, a 2–3, a 1–2, a straight Prep grade and *no problem grades!*

The specialist timetable was arranged so that 'teams' of two class teachers have joint planning time that the VP can also share in. A major part of the VP's role is to support the class teachers — especially in the 5–6 area, since that had initially appeared to be the area of greatest need.

All the multi-age groups are running smoothly. The atmosphere in the school is one of cheerful co-operation. There is growing involvement between classes. Having another pair of hands — the VP's — to call on is increasingly appreciated. A sense of team is appearing among the staff members. The two Grade 5–6 teachers have become largely 'self-supporting' and don't require extra support to the extent that the administration at first felt they would.

Organisational change may be just the thing to make that definable difference between 'good' and 'bad' grades, between a happy school or a not-so-happy school. In our case, it worked.

M.M.

Supporting relief (and first-year) teachers
ETs — it can be a hard day's pay

In Victoria (Australia) relief teachers are aptly named 'emergency teachers'; at times of sickness, stress or the 'day-off', in comes the ET loaded up with 'gear' to fill the breach. Unfortunately, ET's are sometimes treated with low regard by full-time staff and the students as not being 'real' teachers. They may be perceived as having lower status both in and out of the classroom; the students may even resent their being there instead of their own teachers. Witness the playground duty situation: 'You're not a real teacher here. You can't tell us what to do!' Yet we all rely on their services, and most do a good job under quite difficult conditions.

- They have to fill in and establish quickly the rapport that the full-time teacher has developed over time. This is particularly acute in the learning of names and special or idiosyncratic routines of that class, and it can create some stress for the relieving teacher.

- They are often tested out by the hard or reputation classes, who may in fact be the reason the regular teacher is taking a day off.
- They may be coming into situations where little preparation or support is forthcoming for their work there that day.

What the school can do

It is important that the school communicates to relief teachers that they, too, are valued members of the team — not 'just ETs'.

- A welcome and a brief tour of the relevant parts of the school can be helpful (toilets, photocopier, office-staff, working area, staff room and the protocol involving cups and equipment — and for primary teachers, the location of specialist areas. A map of the school won't go astray, either.
- They should each be given a copy of the timetable and yard-duty roster.
- Any medical information required at primary level (including medicine to be given out) should be noted in the class roll — clearly.
- The times for lessons, recess breaks and so on should be made clear — schools vary.
- Exit and time-out procedures should be explained — also who to refer particularly disruptive students to and who the reference-support person is.
- If particularly difficult students are on special behaviour contracts, it may be advisable to make a note of them. One teacher told me that she had a special 'contract' for a Grade 6 boy who had anger-management problems; it involved the boy walking out of the room for a 3–5 minute breather, but this only occurred a few times a week. The supply teacher was not informed and when the boy 'just walked out' the supply teacher challenged, argued and chased him, creating unnecessary conflict that day.

While all this sounds obvious, I've been in a number of schools where little or none of these issues are observed. It can help if the school has a folder containing these key points, to be given to a relief teacher upon arrival.

What the relief teacher can do

It is also helpful for the relief teacher to be prepared — thoughtful preparation can re-duce stress.

Arrive early where possible, introduce yourself, get a copy of the roll and ask 'dumb' questions rather than make assumptions. What about the timetable? Where's the office? Can I use the photocopier (any protocol)? What are the recess times? (Schools vary.) At primary level: Do I escort the students to the specialist teacher? Does the school have a discipline policy? Do the students line up or go straight in? How do I exit a particularly disruptive student and to whom?

Be prepared to do yard duty. Schools often use relief teachers as additional yard supervisors. Schools also have timetable changes — it's an occupational hazard when permanent staff are away.

Have prepared some standard lessons that you know 'work' in case the teacher hasn't left anything (or has left some obscure lesson plan). Some maths/language games and activities, some

'busy' work, some tested stories or books can be helpful, even up to Year 7 or 8. Take a tape recorder for a music activity in lower primary (with rhymes, songs, chants). Learn names quickly and use them each time you address a student. If uncertain of them, ask. If you are given an obviously dummy name, either use it or say 'I'll check that later'. Avoid stupid arguments or providing an audience. If time, a seating plan, with names, can help — or during on-task time as you move around the room ask a student who 'the girl with the green jumper' (for example) is, then go and address her: 'How's it going there, Kylie? Can I see your work, thanks?'

Have a copy of 'your own' rules with you. Prepare a chart (large enough to see from the back of the room) with a key heading prefacing every rule (and one or two points about each one):

Our treatment (or manners) rule

Our communication (or talking) rule

Our learning (or work) rule

Our safety rule

Our movement rule (this covers toilet as well)

These few rules need to be discussed briefly at the start of the day (or lesson). Be positive. 'It's nice to be working with you today. My name is Mr Rogers. I know you've got your class rules, and I've brought the ones I use — as you can see, mine are not much different from your teacher's.' Direct a student whose name you know to put them up. 'David, I'd like you to put this rule chart up for me. Ta, there's Blu-tack on the back.' Keep talking, and demonstrate a positive expectation. If you get the rare 'No' or 'Why should I?', put it up yourself in a relaxed, OK manner. 'OK, I'll put it up. Now, have a look up here at ...'. Assume that you, with them, will have a good day.

Briefly discuss what is meant by each rule. For example, under the heading 'communication rule' (or 'talking rule' for lower primary), the key points can be briefly (and neatly) written.

• Hands up, one at a time, without calling out.

• Quiet working noise, thanks.

Under the 'manners rule':

• Speak politely, thanks (no put-downs).

• Ask to borrow, to put things back, to take turns.

• Use one another's first names.

• Use the words 'please', 'thanks', 'can I borrow?'.

Of course, having a rule and enforcing it are two different things. As soon as Nick or Paula calls out, give a firm (but controlled, even pleasant) rule reminder: 'Paula, hands up without calling out, thanks', or 'We've got a rule for asking questions — use it, thanks, Paula'.

If she argues: 'But we can call out in our class — humph!'. Use the redirective skill discussed on pages 37, 45.

TEACHER: Maybe you can call out in your class, but this is the rule we're using today.

STUDENT: It's a dumb rule!

TEACHER: Maybe you think it is — but it's the rule we're using today.

Then resume quickly, confidently, the flow of the lesson or activity. If she still argues, use the 'simple' or 'deferred choice' with known consequences. In short, have a discipline plan alongside your lesson plan (chapter 4).

Be prepared to keep students back briefly to follow up an incident or establish a 'consequence chain'. That is, refer to their regular teacher or year-level form co-ordinator. Avoid nagging; go back to the rule that was broken and ask what is needed to fix things up. If time permits (age-related), students could fill in the three W's:

What happened? (Your version or right of reply.)

What rule (or right) was affected by your behaviour?

What do you need to do to fix things up?

It might be wise to check at the outset the protocol for keeping a student back — whether demerit, detention or referral processes are involved.

If the class is really disastrous, do not hesitate to call for help. Do this even if it means walking across to a colleague and handing him or her a brief note. Some schools have backup plans for reputation classes.

If this occurs at primary level, it may help to run a circuit-breaking activity based on class rewards (Rogers 1990, chapter 7).

When you leave, thank the class — if it went OK. At least say goodbye (for now?). Leave the room as tidy as you found it (tidier, if appropriate). Put yourself in their teacher's place; nobody wants a 'reputation'. If relief teaching is your livelihood, it can be helpful to do small things:

- Clean the white/black boards.
- Leave a copy of your lesson or sheets for the teacher's work program.
- Mark students' work.
- Make sure there is no litter.
- Put books away.
- See that pencils are sharpened (by monitors at lower primary).

If any 'issue' has cropped up with a student, leave a note on the desk or with the co-ordinator.

Leave your relief-teaching number. You'll probably get more work!

Developing a supportive playground management policy

An effective management plan for playground behaviour needs to be supportive for teachers and students alike. It involves, like all discipline and management, a balance of preventative, corrective and supportive procedures.

Preventative procedures

I was working (doing playground duty) in a high school as a consultant during one of Melbourne's uncomfortable winters. I noticed as I walked around that seats were rare. I spoke to several senior students huddled in a concave corner of a building.

'Where are all the seats?' I asked naively.

'What seats? There's none round here ...!'

In one school I observed several badly broken seats that were positively dangerous; bits of jagged wood protruded. When I spoke to the principal about it, he said: 'Oh, we'll get round to it some time!' (and to the small piles of broken concrete around the school; the rubbish, obviously there for some time, banked up against the chain-wire fence; the light hanging off the wall? There was a pervading sense of jadedness). Coming back six months later, I found that the seats were still the same. This communicates a clear message to students and the wider community.

It should be considered essential to provide basic things such as:

- adequate, decent seating;
- trees and shrubs, especially shade trees (even potted shrubs or plants);
- safe playground equipment and areas;
- a set of clear, known, fair, enforced rules;
- games areas, on asphalt and grass, clearly marked out;
- discussion with the student council about playground areas and other issues with each classroom, home-room or form teacher exploring issues relevant to the playground.

We can create a positive playground atmosphere that can reduce stress and improve community tone by demonstrating that we care, as a school community, for our environment.

Corrective action

Inevitably, when we're on playground duty we will face litterbugs, the more hostile swearing incidents (do we close our ears at the passing four-letter provocateurs?), smoking abuse, toilet incidents, unsafe play and bullying. Little wonder that in some schools playground duty is the least pleasant of our responsibilities; especially on those cold days when the north wind blows.

- What do we do when faced with blatant litter dropping?
- What do we say when Jason is teasing Maria?
- How do we manage the crowd scene at a fight?
- What do we do when two Grade 4 girls come up to us and say, crying: 'Damien has, has — anyway, he has stolen our ball!' or 'Michael's taken my bat' or 'Vanessa's buried my doll in the sandpit ... wahhh!'.

Because these issues affect the stress level of all staff, and because we all need support, staff need time to:

- clarify what the current playground issues are regarding discipline;
- clarify rules and consequences;
- prioritise areas of need;
- develop more effective management processes for periods on playground duty);
- develop a workable time-out policy to support staff and students alike.

Policy review

We normally set aside three or four staff meetings to explore playground management.

Before the meetings

Prior to the first meeting, we encourage staff to obtain data on what concerns them about management discipline in the playground. Each staff member records incidents of concern, where they occurred, their frequency and seriousness and the ages and names of students involved. All staff are also requested to fill in two questionnaires (see appendixes IV, V) and to discuss playground issues with their students (both preventative issues and abusive-behaviour issues). Staff also note what they understand are the present:

- playground rules and consequences;
- playground time-out provisions.

The first meeting

At this meeting, staff work in small task groups to clarify the following points.

- What are our current playground rules? Often these need to be reordered into positive expectations that outline responsible behaviours.
- If a rule is going to be useful (as with classroom rules), it needs to be discussed ('owned'), clear, fair, enforceable and enforced (backed up with clear consequences). A small number of rules are arguably easier to manage.
- Normally rules will cover issues like treatment of one another, safety and designated play and eating areas. (Staff may want to add property issues as well.)

Ultimately, rules go back to central rights and responsibilities: 'I have a right to play in a safe environment. I have a right to feel safe at school. I have a right to have my property/ person respected. We have a responsibility to care for one another and the environment'.

Having discussed this issue with countless students, I feel that they are often unclear about what the rules actually are. Staff will need to access their understanding (and misunderstanding) as part of this review.

In time, the revised rules will be published and distributed to each class or year group. If the students feel they have 'owned' the process, then enforcement/consequences are easier to apply. An example of a primary school playground plan is set in appendixes IV, V.

All these rights, of course, have cognate responsibilities for students and staff alike.

Subsequent meetings

The meetings that follow will clarify the data about incidence of misbehaviour. A small-group activity (with whole-group prioritising of outcomes) will note how often bullying or serious fighting occurs, how often it is necessary to address litter, swearing, spitting, teasing and so on.

We can often group behaviours under key areas of concern (such as fighting, no-ball and out-of-bounds areas, abuse, teasing and unsafe play) and then note the frequency and seriousness of each, which age groups most often match such behaviours and where they tend to occur in the playground.

Maintaining consistency

To increase consistency of corrective action by staff, it is important to discuss more effective management/discipline practice.

If, when Damien (Damien again!) is playing in a no-ball area, one teacher yells:'Oi, get out of there with your ball!', another tries to reason, yet another has a long-winded historical debate about play boundaries and still another ignores the offence, students will receive mixed messages.

If we accede to tale-telling: 'Robin stole my ball!' — if we march over and demand it back for Robin's victim — the 'victim' learns little about controlling property rights.

If we argue with students, especially with the 'playground lawyer', we'll often provide an unnecessary audience.

Staff are encouraged to discuss their characteristic strategies in small groups (perhaps of five); they explain how effective they believe such strategies are and whether they enable students:

(a) to respond to the clear rights focus (for treatment and safety);

(b) to 'own' their behaviour — to understand that they are responsible for their behaviour, and can be held accountable.

A good deal has been said about the pointlessness of arguing, so teachers can benefit from exploring ways in which they can develop a playground discipline plan that:

- is set out from least intrusive to most intrusive;
- addresses the behaviour that is infringing fair rules;
- keeps 'confrontational heat' down;
- addresses behaviour ownership and consequences.

For example, faced with a student who says: 'Someone stole my ...', we might use a questioning approach: 'I can see you are upset ('I' message). What are you going to do about it?'. (This is said supportively, but not acceding to the sibilant whine.) 'Dunno.' 'Well, I'll be coming around this same spot in a few minutes. See if you and Maria can come up with a plan, and let me know.'

If the two do come back with a plan, you might help them to assess it, while walking along, to see if it's viable, seeking to encourage them to feel ownership. 'What might happen if you ...? What do you think so and so might do?'

If it's a more serious matter you might want to intervene, or to try an approach given to me by a colleague.

Give an 'assertive' line.

'Maria, you say Damien (not Damien again!) took your red ball?'

'Yes.'...(whine, whine)

'I'm going to suggest you walk over to him (Maria and I can see Damien in the middle distance about 20 metres away) and say, with your hand outstretched like this: "Damien, I want my ball back now, thanks". Say it strong, just like I did. C'mon, show me.' Maria repeats this, but with eyes down, in a 'mousy' voice.

'What do you think Damien will do if you say it like that?' Here I reproduce the *tone*, while she looks at my 'mirroring'. 'OK, I'll watch you go, but you have to do it. I'll stay over here and watch.'

She goes over, and from the distance Damien sees me casually looking at him, looking at her, looking at him ... he decides 'What the heck!' and gives the ball back. If this approach is successful (and many of my colleagues also use this in the classroom with 'victims'), it teaches Maria and Damien something about mutual rights and empowering speech. I might walk past Damien and simply say, 'I'm glad you gave it back'. No more.

If it is noted by teachers that Damien is repeatedly snatching, then we have a longer term problem on our hands and the solution is dealt with on that basis.

There are other possibilities. We call Damien aside and question him. We give Damien a choice. 'Damien, it's been reported that you've taken Maria's ball.'

'I haven't, s'lie!'

'If you have, I'm asking you to return it or I may have to ask you to stay back at afternoon play to discuss it with me and Maria.'

'S'lie!'

We don't argue. We walk away, leaving him with a choice.

What we're seeking to do, then, is develop a workable, short-term interactive discipline plan for the playground.

It will explore the way we use directions, deal with argumentative, rebellious students, and remind or restate rules when this short-term plan will discuss 'the more effective thing to say and do when ...'.

It will also suggest how to put ownership back to the students, from giving them simple choices through to considering consequences.

What we normally come up with is a plan for each of the key management areas:

- dealing with bullying, fighting, violence and verbal abuse;
- dealing with blatant litter-dropping as well as residual litter;
- dealing with unsafe and out-of-bounds play behaviours;
- dealing with swearing, teasing, tale-telling;
- dealing with students arguing among themselves, as in 'game' situations.

Assuming teachers are fair and are neither provocative nor unnecessarily petty, students ought to be expected to follow their reminders or directions. Experience shows, however, that a significant number of students feel the need to argue or grandstand. The skills of redirecting and giving clear choices need to be discussed regarding misbehaviour of low seriousness.

For example, if students are playing in an area reserved for Preps, will we simply remind them and question them ('Where are you supposed to be playing' or 'Do you know the playground rule for this area?') or will we give them a 5-minute sit-out in the time-out area?

We'll need to discuss when we apply consequences such as time-out.

This management plan, or discipline plan, serves as a *recommended line of practice* to both permanent and temporary staff.

It is worth inviting parents to this — as, indeed, to any — policy review, as it is an area of key concern for their children. The ongoing policy, like all management policy, seeks to enhance the rights of all by clarifying the responsibilities of all in a supportive context. It also needs to be balanced by considerations about the quality of the environment children play in — including provision of ample litter bins with wind-proof lids! (see the staff question-naire in appendix V). The policy, especially the time-out component, needs to be published and distributed to all staff and made available (either complete or in a summary) to parents.

Use of time-out in the playground

There are some behaviours that clearly demand the use of time-out in the playground:

- bullying;
- significant fighting (as distinct from silly play-fighting, which needs to be redirected);
- significant breaches of safety and boundary rules;
- persistent non-compliance with reasonable teacher direction.

Because playground supervision involves all staff, use of time-out support needs to be a whole-school issue. Along with the management plan, staff need to develop a consistent time-out policy communicated to all members of the school community.

Rationale

Parents and students will know that significant abuse of safety or treatment rights cannot be tolerated: violence, unsafe behaviour and abuse are non-negotiable. Time-out in the playground, as in the classroom, has to be seen as a logical and reasonable consequence of misbehaviour, as well as a community sanction.

Teachers need to know they will be supported by the senior management in dealing with serious breaches of playground rules.

The management team will need to develop, with staff, a workable time-out system.

Playground and classroom are seen by students as 'separate' arenas, and the last thing a teacher wants to hear is: 'Your student, Damien, was in trouble at lunch recess'. When 'my' students are in the playground, they are everybody's management responsibility. This is an important point; while it may be helpful to know that Damien has been in trouble, it is the school's responsibility during recess to deal with the disruption *at that time*. Again, this point needs to be discussed with all staff.

The questions we've discussed in many schools when developing a time-out policy are these:
- What sorts of behaviours will occasion time-out? How can we be consistent about this?
- Where will students be directed to go to for time-out?
- What if a student refuses to go to a 'time-out seat' or 'time-out room'?
- What about senior staff's involvement (especially if a time-out room is opted for)?
- When will parents be notified?
- What will be the role of class, form or home-room teacher?
- How long will the child be expected to remain in time-out? — variable time depending on seriousness or at duty teacher's discretion?
- If a room is opted for, will it operate for all time-out across the school or just at lunch recess and classroom exit times?
- What sort of monitoring records will be kept?

All these questions form part of the review of playground management policy.

Many schools I've worked with operate a 'cascade' policy.

1   A playground seat, called a 'time-out seat' (for primary schools) or 'cool-off seat' is used for less serious breaches of playground rules.

2   The student is sent or escorted to the office for more serious behaviour (blatant refusal to follow teacher direction, or aggressive, violent behaviours).

3   All time-out incidents are recorded in the 'playground time-out monitoring book'. If more than three records of minor time-out, or 'the bench', are noted, parents are called up to work with staff. If there are more than two serious breaches, parents are notified, and in the case of a third, there is the possibility of suspension.

   As soon as teachers come off duty, they record (in the monitoring book) the date and time of the breach and the student's name, if known — a photo listing in the staff room is an excellent idea, indicating grades, rooms and teachers. The incident is then followed up by senior staff.

4   A card system is used for non-compliant students, those who refuse to go to 'the bench' or 'office' or who are 'uncontrollable'. A card (say a red card) is carried on duty; if a level 2 incident (see above) is in force, the card is sent to the office via a safe student (or two) to enlist immediate staff support. In smaller schools (primary especially) the card may simply go straight to the staff room, whereupon a member of staff will go out and direct the student calmly, optimistically and firmly to 'come with me to the office now'. (This is similar to the time-out model discussed for classroom use.)

5   If a room is used, especially to deal with the small groups of violent students found in some schools, staff need to discuss a roster system. Obviously the fairest is one in which every staff member (including the principal) takes part.

6   Staff also need to discuss longer term consequences. The key to the success of any time-out policy is to see it as part of a total management policy that has the corrective, consequential discipline balanced by the longer term supportive processes to enable students to enjoy a productive recess time (see appendix II).

Chapter 7

Staff development

Professional development

The professional development of staff is a significant factor in promoting:

- common goals that develop a supportive environment rather than one in which individual teachers 'do their own thing' (however good that thing might be);
- effective practice;
- ideas and practices known to reduce interactive stress (especially better classroom-management skills and better staff communication).

Staff development is about getting the best out of the team that resides at your school. That 'best' involves the range of skills, repertoires, backgrounds, attitudes, beliefs and practices held by that staff. I've been in many classrooms in hundreds of schools, and the tone of the classroom — and of the school — is significantly affected by that interaction between beliefs and practices.

... of the last thirteen years of my teaching, I look back to the first eight with satisfaction, the last five with sadness. The difference between these two periods doesn't really relate to major differences in the type of kids ... I have always worked in the 'rougher' areas of the western suburbs of Melbourne. What was different was the atmosphere of the school — in particular, the support and camaraderie of the staff and the genuine concern of the principal for the staff.

It strikes me as comic, on reflection, how many times I have sat on committees and written up lovely ideals about pupil self-esteem, encouragement of pupils and effective conflict resolutions — often this was done in a staff room where people were divided by fear or resignation. We were meant to develop these positive aims for students in an atmosphere of destructive staff morale.

Joy

For example, a dominance belief — children (and staff) must respect me and my position (status) — often creates stress. Witness the senior staff member telling a colleague he (or she) must have the report in by Friday or ... 'Telling', especially when the voice tone is harder, spatial proximity closer and a clear message conveyed that 'I don't really like or respect you', often creates conflict — in peer and student alike. This style of management is not merely different; it springs from a 'working belief' about the nature and kind of control.

If I tell Jason in Grade 5 in a bossy 'way' to get back to his seat, it is not merely a reaction to his wandering, it is a statement of what I believe about how to manage children: 'I must control him — I therefore must tell him "Get back to your seat now!"' Function and belief coalesce with spatially close presence and waved finger. Such practices (especially with hostile students) 'create' the arguments and conflicts that often ensue, so student interaction and learning and the classroom tone is affected. I need to add here again that I'm not talking about the occasional angry outburst we often have with our students, or about justifiable anger, but about 'characteristic' belief seen in 'characteristic' work practices.

The question is, how can we work with 'high-demand' teachers to improve a more positive management and teaching style? Or with the teacher whose verbal repertoire clearly communicates indecision and non-assertion?

Identifying skills

One way of improving classroom practices is to identify appropriate or desirable skills within guiding management principles.

The questions we ask, therefore, are these.

1 What are our overall objectives in classroom management (for both teaching and learning, as well as for social interaction)?

2 What sorts of skills are we looking at that will enable us to work towards these objectives?

3 Can we identify areas in our practice where we believe changes can be or need to be made?

4 Within the support processes of department, faculty or team, are we willing to work in a collegial support group? Emphasise that the purpose of the group (faculty or cross-faculty) is to increase our professional skills in the area of managing classroom behaviour.

As a feature of this school's continuing professional development, we are inviting staff to develop teaching and learning teams (small groups of peers within grade levels, across grade levels, subject- or faculty-based, or based around common interests).

Peer-support groups

The benefits of peer-support groups at our school have been:

- confidence, enjoyment and pride in one's profession — that is, being a teacher;
- the development of the qualities of enthusiasm, optimism and persistence, with staff preparing to take the leadership roles;
- the emergence of a strong group of teachers who are now interested in both the classroom and the running of the school;
- security, [the] feeling of not being isolated but of [the] group sharing [and] being able to discuss real discipline problems without fear of criticism, and finding workable solutions.

Jan (a senior high school teacher)

Using a small-group (peer-support) model, we identify key skills as targets for individuals to work on in their classrooms, then later use peer or mentor feedback (in groups or even in classroom peer coaching) to fine-tune those skills. As stated earlier, if this approach to professional development is going to work it has to be seen by teachers as having practical, useful outcomes.

Personal (interaction) skills

Characteristic use of children's names
These are used even in discipline contexts.

Generally positive tone in language interaction
This is difficult to quantify except by conscious awareness, but it can be seen in use of language and spatial presence.

Directional language
- 'Pen down, thanks' to a noisy 'tapper' rather than 'Don't tap with that pen!'
- 'Facing the front and listening' rather than 'Don't talk when I'm talking!'
- 'When you've put the maths equipment away, you can read in the library corner', rather than 'No, you can't go in the library corner because you haven't put the blocks away!'

Conscious addressing of behaviour, not the student
- 'I don't like it when you're rude like that' or 'We have a classroom rule about helpful language. Use that, thanks'.
- 'Hands up without calling out' rather than 'Don't call out! I'm sick of it, d'you hear?'

Conscious eye-scanning of the room
This is especially useful when tactically ignoring and when 'up-front'.

Development of a clear, assertive, tone in speaking
The voice sounds decisive, expectant and certain rather than indecisive, victimish, unsure or aggressive, harsh and hectoring. One way to achieve this is to practice with a colleague or in a small-group context to get a 'balance'. Another way is to use a tape recorder for personal or collegiate 'evaluation.'

Ability to keep the flow in a lesson delivery
This involves being able to dip in and out in our up-front management. If two students are talking in a distracting way, a directional reminder is better than a confrontational, close-proximity/overdwelling dialogue or argument. 'Denise, Michelle, I want you to face the front and listen, thanks.'

The teacher then goes back to the lesson, directs a question to another student or goes back to the chalkboard or demonstration, keeping a 'flow'. He or she also by turning away to 'pick up' another student demonstrates an *expectation* of compliance — does not demand it or plead for it (Rogers 1990).

Movement/proximity awareness
Effective teachers are aware of personal space and move in and out of students' spatial area respectfully, even when they have to confront misbehaviour such as defiance.

Walking near Jason's desk, and alongside, with a confident 'Can I see your work, thanks, Jason?', and waiting those few seconds for the eye-contact response that effectively says 'yes' before reaching out to turn the book towards you — this is eminently better than just taking the book with an off-the-cuff remark: 'Is this the best you can do?' or 'What did I tell you to do, eh?'. Some teachers are clearly not aware of the effect of their general invasive tone and spatial presence on students.

All these skills require, of course, an awareness of the shape of the skill in general and the parts in particular. Once we have noted an area — say, directional language — we can consciously plan to use simple directions that address students to expected or desired behaviours.

Key organisational skills

These skills cover room planning and the organisation of the many elements that make up a teaching and learning environment. They include:

- organising clear, fair, positive, enforceable rules;
- communication to the class of rights and responsibilities (what we ought to expect in our room if we are going to work well together);
- arranging seating plans — stable? rows? mixed tables? mixed gender seating? variable seating according to teaching/learning at the time?
- resources planning (work stations, places for notes from home, lunch-money retrieval, work to be handed in, procedures for pencil sharpening (or not) — in fact, all the 'smooth-running' processes.

As the process develops, teachers — within their peer-support teams — can develop curriculum issues:

- mixed-ability teaching;
- group work;
- co-operative learning;
- work-required assessment in which students contract and 'own' work task goals and process goals (see especially Jones & Tucker 1990).

The emphasis right through any professional development program, whatever the area being considered, is that change is best developed in a supportive context, with our peers, on the job.

Levels of skill awareness and development

While some teachers seem to have natural skill (are they born with it, perhaps?), most of us have to learn the many skills that make up effective teaching and that include:

- time and workload management;
- organisation of space and work areas (for example, seating, work stations and routines such as pencil sharpening, handing out and receiving work);
- planning of the curriculum and assessment of students' work;

- and the big one — management of the behaviour of students, of the twenty-five to thirty moving in and around a small room — seeking to engage them in effective learning while attending to social dynamics!

Teachers may be handicapped by poor university or college training regarding classroom management/discipline, or by having little experience of working with children or attitudes that are unrealistic, such as that children *must* obey teachers, *must* respect them, *must* do as they are told the first time, or that 'I *must* be liked and respected and listened to or I am not a good teacher'. This is what Karen Horney (1945) calls the 'tyranny of the shoulds'. This high-demand thinking can block effective emotional coping, self-management and the ability to manage others effectively.

Some teachers say that it's all up to personality as to how well we teach and manage. While not denying the special place of a sense of humour, an easygoing nature and the 'kind and thoughtful teacher' approach, there are definite skills one can learn to enhance whatever 'personality' we have. Some teachers — those who dislike children or find it very difficult to like them, and who find a multi-task profession like teaching very difficult to manage — may well consider this profession not for them. But most of us want to improve our relationship-building skills. Human relations are the essence of our profession, from the principal 'down' to the teacher enabling a Year 8 class to understand the benefits of salad and how to concoct one, or the Prep teacher sitting with twenty-odd children and introducing concepts through literature. There are skills involved in relating to and managing others as well as in teaching place value, or acids and bases.

- How can I correct disruptive behaviour without being bossy, argumentative or pleading?
- How can I avoid getting bogged down in meaningless discussions about chewing gum and comics?
- How can I increase student on-task time?
- How can I direct students to 'own' their own behaviour?
- How can I be corrective and supportive as a teacher?
- How can I reduce the levels of noise in my room?
- And how can I do all this when my insides are signalling frustration, arrogance — even anger?

These are questions one often asks about management, but similar questions can be asked about curriculum, group approaches to learning and playground management.

These questions may be relating to significant skill development or improvement of existing skills as well as to stress management. What I've noticed with teachers in professional development, or with teachers in training, is that people often vary in the levels of awareness of their skills and of how consciously they apply them. These levels may broadly be termed around the degree of consciousness of personal and group effectiveness — an effectiveness that is not merely utility, but is effectiveness in reaching value-invested goals of teaching, learning and management.

1 unconscious ineffectiveness
2 conscious ineffectiveness
3 'connecting the skill' — approximating 'known' to 'actual'
4 conscious effectiveness
5 unconscious effectiveness

If we apply this working principle of developmental skill to, say, classroom management, we find the same pattern.

This 'developmental awareness' in one's skill and its usage holds true in any area. When I first began sailing, I was motivated by the Arthur Ransome children's stories (about children sailing on English lakes and rivers). Motivation and a need to try it, or want to try it, coalesced. It looked so easy and graceful; yet when I first got into a boat the wind, the rudder, the ropes (mainsail it's called for some unusual reason) all seemed unnatural — even uncomfortable. But I persevered and practised. While I was 'consciously' ineffective, that was OK; I knew that in any skill one is often at a 'natural' handicap, and although some of my peers 'connected' the skill more rapidly than I, I persevered. I was shown the skill in whole and in part, and encouraged to keep at it. It would come. After much practice I became more confident, more aware, more efficient, until I could be described as generally, consciously efficient. To be honest, I am not at that level of sailing skill where I am unconsciously effective, but who knows ...? I rarely hit other boats!

1 Unconscious ineffectiveness

There are some teachers who are clearly having significant management/discipline problems but who are either unaware of their inefficiency or are denying it.

Denial that one is ineffective may arise from fear of rejection or misunderstanding by others. I've worked with many teachers who are clearly ineffective in classroom management but whose self-esteem cannot and will not embrace the willing support of others. A common 'discount hierarchy' heard is (a) 'Well, that doesn't describe me!' (denial of existence of inefficiency); (b) 'Well, what I do doesn't hurt them! Anyway, it works' (utility — this attitude does not rate as significant the current inefficient practice); (c) 'Well, I wasn't trained. It's too hard to do what you're doing — it wouldn't work, anyway'. Until one is aware of the need for change and couples it with a willingness to change one's practice, little effective improvement can take place.

However, a staff workshop or in-service on classroom management that stresses a peer-support model for skill development has often seen a significant shift to acknowledgment of 'conscious' ineffectiveness. This, coupled with a program for professional development, can see significant improvement in classroom practices.

2 Conscious ineffectiveness

This occurs when our cognition and will are challenged by experience ('I've just got to handle this differently; it can't go on like this') or information (we read about a different approach, or see it, or are in-serviced).

The sorts of questions we ask ourselves are these.

- Do I need this skill, comparing it with my present practice? Is it of value to me?
- Who can I go to for help?
- What sort of skills do I need?
- What is the 'shape' of the skill?
- What does it look and sound and feel like?

Skills are definable (even relational skills).

Take the skill of speaking positively, clearly and directionally when you are correcting misbehaviour.

I noticed in my own practice, and with colleagues who asked me to observe and give feedback on theirs, that we tended to speak in the negative and often too spatially close to the child.

For example, if a student is calling out, what is the point of merely saying, 'Don't call out!' in a loud voice? Particularly if we also move too close and add, with outstretched, pointing finger: 'I'm sick and tired of telling you — you always call out in my class ...'. If we characteristically tell students 'not to' or 'don't' when correcting them, the interactive and relational tone is unnecessarily negative. Of course, personal stress levels come into this; it is not just skill, but a conscious skill change can increase a sense of coping.

If we speak directionally: 'David, hands up, thanks', adding a non-verbal 'hand up' as a kind of privately understood message, the tone is more positive while still remaining correctional.

The broad shape of the actual skill is the 'language' of direction:
- 'Facing the front and listening, Damien — thanks.'
- 'Pen down, Michael, I'm teaching.'
- 'Sean, do me the courtesy of facing the front and listening — and comic away, thanks.'
- 'I want you to go back to your seat, Michelle' (or 'I expect you to ...') rather than 'Why are you always out of your seat?'
- 'When you're back in your seat, then I'll come over to mark your work, Paul', rather than 'Don't get out of your seat — I've told you before!'

While this may sound like common sense (and I could give scores of examples), my experience is that many teachers speak more easily in the negative. While command language ('don't', 'stop!') is fine for the safety or aggression situation, it is not necessary for most of our corrective discipline and mostly occurs because of frustration and an unreflective verbal repertoire.
- 'David, use the scissors safely, like this' or even 'David how are you supposed to use the scissors?' is better than merely 'Don't ...' or 'How many times have I told you...!'.

To speak *directionally* (to behaviour we want to see or 'ought' to see within a responsible classroom) is not easy. For many it is an *acquired skill*.

It also involves other elements, such as:
- tone of voice (clear, firm but not aggressive, whining or pleading: try giving the above directions in a sarcastic, loud or petulant and whining voice — it changes the nature of the message);
- a confident body language (not slumped with that vacant, indecisive sighing or the tense, hostile 'You threaten me!' pose);
- reasonable proximity (especially when teaching 'up front') — not too close or over-bearing;
- showing we expect compliance by not overdwelling, but rather giving the direction and then moving on to the on-task students or, if up front, going back to the lesson itself.

All these micro skills help to balance the whole skill, and one way to assess how effectively one communicates that is through peer feedback, or even role-play.

At a number of universities in Australia (and in the UK), I have involved students in classroom-management role-plays. Someone takes the role of 'teacher', the rest of the group role-play a typical 'classroom'. One or two 'students' (or more as time goes by) disrupt, following a scripted card from the facilitator (Rogers 1990, 'Gentle Assertive Role Plays').

The script lists what the disruptor is to say and do, and for how long. This gives control over the role-play.

What my students (teacher-trainees and also experienced teachers) soon realise is that it's one thing to know (cognise) a skill, but quite another to be efficient or effective with that skill.

For example, when we're role-playing, calling out or talking out of turn, the most common disruption (Elton Report 1989), the person role-playing teacher 'knows' the skill of directing simply, briefly and then resuming the lesson, but under pressure of the simulated calling out resorts to a more 'natural' response. 'Why are you calling out?' or a semi-nice plead, 'Please don't call out', or — if they get the language 'right' — 'Jason, hands up, thanks' (then resuming the lesson) may need more assertion in the voice to demonstrate certainty of optimistic response in the direction given.

When you observe someone leading a group (of Preps, Year 10s, Uni. students or ...), the actual message or content is important but can be significantly weighted by the tone — how assertive or aggressive or uncertain it is, how loud or soft, what the body language is, how enthusiastic. So the direction, 'David, I want you to put your food in your bag or on my desk, thanks', spoken while the teacher is moving around the room (marking and encouraging) will be received according to how it is said.

This is a very valuable lesson. In the safety of well-constructed (not free) role-play, my students begin to realise that until a skill is practised and is moving towards a conscious state, it is not really 'known'. One can practise the other elements of the skill, even in a 'mechanical' way (Johnson & Johnson 1989), until one feels comfortable and reasonably natural.

3 Connecting the skill — approximating 'known' to 'actual'

It's one thing to practise the skill privately (even cognitive rehearsal, saying it aloud in your head, is advantageous) or with colleagues, but it's another thing to practise it back in room 17. The main thing is to stay with it. If we start a thing and merely give up because it's too hard to remember to say this or do that or act this way, the problem can hardly be said to be the skill area itself. Effort, exercise of will and practice will see improvement (not perfection); if we 'fail' (shout or argue with the student) we can always work on it, or improve next time.

It may even be stressful at this stage merely because we are consciously seeking to effect different or new ways of thinking and behaving. This uncomfortable feeling of 'it's not fully me' is normal.

'Failure' is part of the process. It actually means that we're learning, our skill is still developing. What it doesn't mean is that we are failures.

One way to improve in the connective phase is to find situations in which we can experience success: the 'safer' students, the easier class or group. Try it out there or with a colleague; ask for feedback. Actually, the feedback from trusted peers can be an invaluable source of encouragement. Our profession sorely lacks collegiate feedback, yet learning theory tells us that encouragement and feedback are essential features of skill development.

One of the students in my tutorial group last year (at university) went out enthused with an approach I call 'Question and feedback' (Rogers 1989,1990), based on the ideas of William Glasser. This is the asking of a direct question, 'What ...?', 'How ...?' or 'When ...?', rather than 'Why are you two talking?' or 'Why are you out of your seat?'

In its very standard form, it looks like this. The teacher walks up to a student, Vincent, apparently wasting time — out of his seat and chatting away to a friend in another seat. The trainee-teacher approached: 'Vincent, what are you doing?' (The teacher was not aggressive; his voice was clear, controlled). The student responded with 'You're the teacher, you tell me!', with a kind of controlled sarcasm. I asked the teacher what he said and did next. 'I dunno. I was stymied! Lost for words.'

My colleague had got the words — even the tone — 'right', but was unprepared for the teacher-baiting that followed.

Redirection is another part of the skill he had not yet developed. To his credit, he went back and worked on the further skills and is now an effective first-year teacher.

4 Conscious effectiveness

TEACHER: David, I notice you haven't started work.

STUDENT: Yeah. (*arms folded sulkily, eyes dropped — all messages of low-level attention-seeking*) Well, this maths is dumb, isn't it!

TEACHER: Maybe you think it is, but it's the work we're doing today. If you need a hand, I'll help.

STUDENT: When am I gonna do dumb vectors?

TEACHER: Maybe never, who knows? It's the work we're doing today, though. Give it your best shot. I'll help if needed. Just ask.

Here the teacher leaves eye-contact and moves off, leaving the student to 'own' his behaviour.

What the teacher has done here *consciously* is to tune-in and redirect. Instead of arguing ('Don't you tell me that this work is dumb — I spent ages preparing this!' or variations on this theme) or pleading ('Well, what *do* you want to do?' — sigh, sigh), the teacher acknowledges the student's words but concentrates on the primary issue. This is a skill and it is not easy.

If I'm teaching up front, from the board, and two students are talking and secretly reading some pop magazine, how I direct and redirect will depend on whether I easily or quickly fall into an argument.

I could say 'Denise, Michelle, I want you to put the comic in the bag and face the front and listen, thanks'.

If, as I turn away from these two students, they have the last word: 'But we're only talking about the work!' (with folded arms, a sulky tone and a grunt or a sigh) and I then say: 'Don't lie to me' (moving close) — you were not talking about the work', I set up a potential pointless argument. Especially with students whose agenda is 'power'.

Or the following exchange could take place.

TEACHER: (*in a tone of uncertainty or indecision*) Girls, why are you reading a comic? Please put it away?

STUDENTS: We weren't, we're only talking about the work, Miss! Geez, we're not the only ones who talk! What about Craig and Sean?

TEACHER: Oh, come on, be reasonable!

It can so easily get out of hand. The ability to redirect is a skill that will lead to a better handling of argument or conflict.

STUDENTS: We're only talking about the work!

TEACHER: Maybe you were, but I want you to face the front and listen, thanks.

This neither says they're lying nor pleads with them; it concentrates on the issue that is important at the time. This skill (redirection) is one that can be applied widely in working with students either in groups or individually.

I was teaching a colleague these skills in a Grade 4 classroom recently. A small, furtive-looking chap didn't want to read during quiet-reading time. I directed him: 'Tim, I want you to get a book and find a place to read quietly' ('I' direction with expectation).

STUDENT: Don't want to read!

TEACHER: Maybe you don't, but I want you to take a book and find a place to read quietly.

STUDENT: I'm bored of reading! (*folded arms and sulky voice*)

TEACHER: Maybe you are bored (*do not at this time ask why — save 'why' questions for longer term management*) but I want you to ...'

At this point, I gestured to a place near the bookcase and walked away, seeking to communicate my expectation. We normally 'walk away' after redirecting three (or no more than four) times. Out of the corner of my eye I saw him slowly move into the corner with a sigh, slumped shoulders and a 'notice me' expression.

W.Rogers.

When recently counselling a father who admitted that he had constant arguments with his teenage daughter, he said this skill (tuning in, then redirecting) was not natural. Of course it isn't. Many skills are not 'natural' or easy in that sense. 'What is natural?' I asked. He looked away, a bit sheepish. 'To argue, I suppose ...'.

We can still legitimise emotion while redirecting; what is really ineffective is to descend into an argument — often a heated and a wasted one — for the sake of it. It takes two to argue, but a conscious skilled awareness to redirect.

5 Unconscious effectiveness

This is the stage at which we don't have to think, *all* the time: 'Am I doing this right? What should I say now? Broadly speaking, the skill becomes second nature. The tone of voice, the body language, the content of what we say in our interactive dialogue is now reasonably natural (on an eight out of ten average!). This is an important stage, and one that assists in stress reduction.

The skill of driving is naturally stressful. When we were first learning there were many skills to master — but given time and 'failure' (naturally occurring failure) we become 'unconscious' about clutch, accelerator, mirror, indicators, braking, gear-changing. If we had constantly to remember those, the act of driving would be so much more stressful. So too is it in management; our 'style' can change to a more assertive, positive style following similar principles.

David is a science/maths teacher. While he is a thoroughly nice bloke, he often got into arguments with his students (especially the Year 9s). After working with me as part of a peer-support team, he began to acknowledge areas of his management that were clearly ineffective. He regularly confronted students with 'Why are you calling out, eh?' or 'Don't keep getting out of your seat'. He was easily sucked into pointless (often silly) verbal exchanges over talkativeness, seat-changing, gum chewing, task-avoidance or calling out.

Together we identified key areas of his practice to work on, and began a process of skill development and behaviour change which in turn saw significant changes in his students' academic and social behaviour.

He was mature enough to say: 'Well, I've been teaching for eight years, but I realise these are areas I need to work on'.

Using peer feedback, he identified areas such as:
- unclear, poorly enforced class rules;
- inconsistent application of consequences (as a colleague of mine says, 'it's the certainty of a consequence, not its severity, that counts');
- a verbal repertoire that tended to be negative and often argumentative;
- mixed messages — when he was angry he communicated only his anger, not the reasons for it;
- threatening rather than making 'options' clear.

He tended also to have poor relational skills arising in part from his stress, 'created' by the students' behaviour, and in part from his increasing anxiety about 'failing'.

Peer support, with a change in classroom practices, saw a much more relaxed and confident teacher.

The last session (a joint teaching session) I had with David was with 'those' Year 9s. We had the students working in small groups of mixed abilities. One of the girls in the group I was working with said: 'Eh Mr Rogers, look at him'. 'Who?' 'Mr ——. Look at him, he's smiling!' 'Oh, come on, Melissa, so he's smiling.' 'Yeah, but he never smiles!' 'Well, it's good then, isn't it? Perhaps you ought to tell him.' She went up to him during the course of the lesson and said: 'Mr Rogers told me to tell you I like you smiling'. She grinned. To his credit, he said: 'Thanks. I'm pleased my smile makes you happy'.

For David, twelve months of peer support on and off, coupled with a conscious skill change, was worth it. And David was an 'experienced' teacher.

More than just 'experience'

I've worked in many, many schools with teachers who act on the assumption that experience alone is what counts. 'I've been teaching for fifteen years' — the hidden agenda being 'I've therefore learned what (even all) I need to know'. This attitude is a hard nut to crack. One can see, from the next classroom, that a teacher's skill repertoire is inefficient, even ineffective — you can hear it!

You hear phrases such as 'You stupid thing! What are you? Haven't I told you before to wipe up the clag? Your table's a disgrace!', 'Jason! Don't call out. When will you learn?!' or 'How can I be expected to be in two places at once!'

Her room is regularly loud, her tone often disrespectful, except when the principal is near. Then she changes her tone, and 'please' and 'thanks' can be heard as well. So she *can* choose to behave differently.

We can change our practice if:
- we believe in what we need and want to change towards — that is, if we believe 'this' is worthwhile;

- we are aware of what the necessary skills are — what they look and sound like;
- we have support in applying those skills to the area of application — in this case, the classroom;
- we make the effort required to change.

Do Bono (1986) makes an interesting point in this regard — it is a fatal mistake to assume that experience is the same as skill or that if a 'skill' is used it must somehow be right because of years of experience in using it. He quotes the example of the two-finger typist (say, journalist) who goes through life with a two-finger repertoire — serviceably, but inefficiently. A typist who has spent, say, six months learning efficient skills and then practising them can with some ease outdistance the two-finger typist with fifteen years' experience.

Do Bono compares this example with that of participants in 'conflict' situations whose years of inefficient conflict-resolution practices may only serve to handle conflict poorly; the 'years of experience' count for little. Skill and experience are clearly not the same thing. Skill at what?

In the classroom-management area even effective teachers may not think of changing both the shape and the reinforcement of rules from negative to positive to improve classroom tone. 'Walk quietly, without running' (a classroom rule) or 'Sean, walking, thanks' is a positive and directional reminder. Many teachers don't think of using something other than 'don't-style' directions — not because they are 'bad' teachers, but because they haven't thought through or seen the need of alternatives. Yet there are alternatives.

Even when I've worked with kindergarten teachers we get better tone and a higher compliance rate when we use 'when/then' directions rather than 'no you can't because' statements.

STUDENT: I wanna play with the jigsaws now
TEACHER: No, you can't, because you haven't put your playdough away.
      or:
      Yes, you can play with the jigsaw *when* you've put the....' or '*When* you've put the ...., *then* you can ....'.

The most talented, 'natural' teachers may need little training or advice because they learn so quickly from experience. At the other extreme there are a few teachers for whom training and advice will not be properly effective because their personalities do not match the needs of the job. It is clear, however, that the majority of teachers can become more effective classroom managers as a result of the right kinds of training, experience and support.

Elton Report, p. 69

Peer feedback and professional development

About eight years ago I began to do something teachers are often loath to do: to invite a colleague — a trusted colleague (c'mon, there must be one out there!) — to come into my classroom and give me some feedback on my discipline/management style (and vice versa).

Well, for the first several visits I passed rather large 'rectal bricks' when he came in (and vice versa) and watched me teach and manage my classes. You see, my self-esteem, in a sense, was on the line.

Teachers tend to be *'professionally private'*. Even though we teach next to or near each other and can often hear our 'struggles' through walls, we rarely go into each other's classes to see if we can effect 'problem solving by analysis and support'.

After a while, it became easier. Like most things (even the dentist!), familiarity can often improve the emotional state and the opportunity to benefit from professional feedback. Anxiety was linked to being thought a 'failure', a 'bad teacher'. What we were doing was not forced on us; we were doing it because we saw a need. We surmised that if we observed what we *actually* said and did we might have a basis for possible, even achievable, change. Some data to work on, as it were.

We picked up a great deal about use of voice, body language, eye-contact and eye-scanning skills, level of assertiveness (as distinct from authoritarian, even aggressive styles of management), rules and how we enforced them, proximity to students during on-task learning time and how we encouraged students and reinforced them. It was illuminating and revealing, and countless teachers have said in retrospect that it was even necessary and worthwhile.

Stephen Colarelli's report (1989) of research in business management may well apply, in principle, to teachers.

- The degree of 'decision making' freedom managers gave workers had a lot more to do with workers' performance than IQ or economic background. (Those decisions are within the policy framework and goals of the group.)
- While it helps to be 'surrounded' by competent managers and motivated co-workers ... *'the crucial element in performance is feedback'* [author's italics]. You need to know how you're doing, ask for feedback from your managers, talk to your co-workers.

We did just that. We then formed interest-based groups of concerned teachers in a number of schools, both primary and secondary (often around discipline, management and curriculum concerns), to discuss our classes, our difficult students, our own feelings about dealing with them, what we believed was working well and what was clearly not working well. We discussed alternative approaches, we read literature on the subject and then tried out new practices in the classrooms. When we took the extra step, however, of going into each other's rooms as observers, we added an important step — *actual* feedback.

In planning peer feedback, there are a number of important considerations.

1 Make a time that suits both of you, within the constraints of timetable and 'free-time'.
2 Decide whether you want a general observation of the lesson or a concentration on specifics such as the up-front phase, the use of directions, whether language is positive or noise-level management. It can help if the observing colleague has a journal in which to record specific dialogue and feelings during class observation, to share later.
3 Remember that the purpose is to observe your colleague's practice in order to give feedback at a later stage. (Make a specific time to do this.)
4 Introduce the colleague (for example, myself) to your class briefly as: 'You know Mr Rogers, he teaches English here. He'll be working with us today'. I then say a brief 'Good morning', no more, and casually wander to the back of the class there to observe the lesson and, most importantly, the interactions between teacher and students — just as he or she will do for me. Most of the teacher classes 'ignore' the visitor provided he or she does not 'scene steal' and stay up front.
5 During the on-task phase of the lesson, as my colleague moves around the room marking, checking, talking, I'll move around keeping my ears and eyes open and observing, too —though not so obviously to students.
6 Over coffee, we'll discuss our findings. This is not easy for either person for the first few times, but the rectal bricks get smaller each time! It's a new way of learning.
7 Decide how long you want to keep the process running. If it's part of a first-year-teacher induction plan, the first three terms can include a fortnightly peer-observation-feedback session. For teachers engaged in an elective program as part of a peer-support program (small groups meeting weekly or fortnightly to discuss common or particular management concerns), peer-observing may occur weekly, fortnightly or as time allows. It is the time factor that is most difficult, apart from the conceptual difficulty of an active collegial observer. (He or she is looking at me!) It's worth noting that the observer learns a great deal, too; because we rarely see teachers teaching (except at assemblies), we can see 'ourselves in others'. A valuable exercise.
8 An alternative to this is the tutor–teacher model in which key teachers act as mentors to model the target skills and to encourage and support their peers as they seek to develop those skills in their classrooms.

Peer support: improving classroom skills through peer observations

Peer support can provide a useful context for the development or improvement of classroom management and discipline skills by collegiate discussion, problem solving, observation and feedback. *Peer observation* is one important feature of peer support, providing useful data to determine how well we're doing and whether we're moving in the direction we want — or need — to go.

The focus of such an approach is professional development; the natural outcome is an increase in teacher confidence and wellbeing, established through a supportive setting for the interchange of concerns, needs and solutions.

Basic assumptions behind the program

We learn best when we feel comfortable about the challenges inherent in new learnings; when the pressure of necessary change (new repertoire) is countered by a *supportive learning environment* — an environment that endorses 'failure' as OK, as a learning process (we note G.K.Chesterton's tongue-in-cheek maxim, 'Nothing succeeds like failure').

Johnson and Johnson (1990) note that participation in collegial support aims at increasing teachers' belief that they are engaged in a joint venture ('We are doing it'), a public commitment to and by the peers to increase their instructional and managerial expertise ('I will try it'), peer accountability ('they are counting on me'), a sense of social support ('they will help and assist me'), a sense of safety ('the risk is challenging, but not excessive') and self-efficacy ('if I make the effort, I will be successful').

It is this balance of personal commitment and support (not authority) that 'energises change efforts by teachers' (pp.1–17).

We learn more effectively when we have the opportunity to see, understand, discuss, contrast and practise new or improved skill repertoires in a controlled environment (peer-support meetings, structured role plays or simulations, and peer-modelling).

To effectively apply new repertoire, to make it 'our own', we need feedback about current practice, and peer observation is one way of gaining such feedback — preferably in the natural (classroom) setting or even in structured, role-play learning settings (Rogers 1990).

- Peer observation is an *elective* feature of peer-support groups designed to foster professional feedback. Any teacher electing to use peer observation/feedback carefully plans, with his or her observing colleague, times of observation and appropriate time and place (not a noisy staff room) for feed-back; how feedback will be given; use of written feedback; how each will be introduced to classes; how best to utilise the feedback.

   It is advisable that peer feedback form part of a peer-support group formed for professional development.

- Peer observation is a *mutual* learning experience between teachers who are amenable to working together and who share a common desire (even need) to improve their classroom management and discipline skills (or any area of professional practice). This is an essential point to note; the object is not merely supervision or appraisal.
- Peer observation is based around peers observing on and reporting on one another's current practice and on attempts at trialling a new skill repertoire.
- It is not a superior–subordinate relationship.
- Peer observation is often part of a wider professional development program that includes in-servicing and workshops on classroom management and discipline skills.

The emphasis of the new or improved repertoire is assertive leadership focusing on the mutual rights of all members of the classroom group.

The feedback in peer observation aims at giving targeted, non-judgmental data to the learner/practitioner about current or trialled practice. The data is drawn from observations that concentrate on:

- room organisation;
- the beginning and ending phases of a lesson;
- general lesson/curriculum organisation and delivery (and the effect on classroom learning and on-task behaviour);
- general and specific verbal skills in discipline transactions.

In peer observation, the observing partner is looking at what is said and how it is said, and the nature and use of directions, statements, questions and so on in discipline/management transactions — also, when and how a teacher enters into a discipline transaction, observing such things as proximity, body language and expectation.

Giving feedback

When giving feedback, peer partners are not judging their colleagues' behaviour, they are *reporting* aspects of it. The reporting (data) forms the basis of a mutual discussion about how the observer felt in the practising teacher's class — what he or she heard and saw. Some of this will be positive, some negative in the sense that the observer is noting and reporting ineffective practice. There is little point in the observer saying 'Dave, it seems like they are a noisy class — you have your hands full there'. The feedback needs to be *specific*: was the teacher effective with directions? Were they positive, clear, brief, targeted, unmixed?

If there are bad habits and inefficient practices, then they can be reported uncritically.
- 'David, when Sean was crawling under the table, it looked like you were tactically ignoring him — were you?'
- 'Were you aware of what you said to Melina when she was out of her seat? No? Well, what you said was ...'.
- 'Dave, can you remember what you said to Michelle when she ...?'
- 'David, this is what I heard you say when Mark and Paul were calling out at the beginning of the lesson...'
- 'How did you feel when...?'
- 'I noticed you walked over several times to Jason when he called out across the room. Were you aware of that?' or 'Did you notice that?' or 'When ...?'

The observer will also note aspects of seating, room layout, utility of classroom rules, use of board space, how the teacher applies consequences and how students enter and leave the room (are those chairs up?).

Reflection and interpretation of the data is important. If I know, for example, that I actually say 'Shh!' twenty-odd times to my Grade 4s while they're on the mat, then I can do something about it. If I am aware that I use characteristic negatives that are probably overreinforcing calling out ('No, don't call out!', 'Why are you calling out? I've told you before, haven't I?'), I can then plan how to use tactical ignoring and brief, simple directions, or to restate/remind via the rules (and so on).

If I know that I speak too long to a discipline transaction, then I can learn to give instructions or directions that are briefer, better targeted, more positive.

Improving current classroom practice

We can really only modify our practice when certain conditions or objectives are met.
- We must know and agree what good practice is (or 'should' be). The skills involved in good practice need to be seen as important and achievable *before* a commitment to change is embarked upon. In what way is this skill important? Why do I need — or should I need — to learn it? (This will be answered partly by school policy and partly by professional values about teaching and learning).
- We must get feedback about what our current practice is, and feedback on how we're going when we trial new repertoire. 'Dave, that tactical ignoring was really effective. I noticed you gave no direct eye-contact to Sean; your initial simple direction was brief, spot on. Sounded clear, assertive, but still positive — you used the brief 'thanks' at the end...'.

- Feedback is a supportive and corrective (but not judgmental) process. It enables teachers to assess and to fine-tune a particular skill, process, procedural or organisational requirement. Once the goals of good practice are outlined, with some timeline for their mastery, feedback can enable them to be compared with the target goals — even of specific skills such as the use of direct and indirect questions. Feedback can include both peers keeping a journal, using self-reporting checklists ('How many times did Jason call out? At what point in the lesson? What did I do?') and personal post-observation feedback over a cuppa in a relaxed setting.
- Because any new skill requires practice, there will be mistakes, mistargeting and so on. This is acknowledged (laughed over, even), both in the one-to-one peer context and in the small-group peer context. It is also important for leaders to model — the self-confidence required to lead comes from trying, failing, learning from mistakes and trying again' (Johnson & Johnson 1990, p.1:23).

  New skills require behaviour change — sometimes quite significant change. A new skill will feel unnatural until it becomes characteristic repertoire, and this is where supportive feedback is extremely helpful in providing the mutual motivation inherent in new learning.
- What we are seeking to communicate through the peer-feedback process is a cluster of achievable management/discipline skills, which require conscious appraisal of verbal repertoire and body language. Developing the characteristic nature of a skill will need a conscious preparation of 'what to say when' and 'in what circumstances' prior to the use of such a skill in the classroom setting.

  This can be expressed as a 'discipline or management plan'. Again, an effective plan requires effective preventative and supportive measures as well as the on-task management and discipline measures. With our peers, we can develop a more consciously targeted plan.

It takes effort and practice to learn to give and receive feedback (of both kinds); it takes a degree of maturity to see its usefulness in terms of our professional development. In the form we have discussed it, it has been our experience that such peer feedback is an invaluable source of personal and professional growth.

Summary

Teachers are at various levels in terms of skill repertoire. To develop one's skills, it is important to be conscious of and convinced of the need to do something about them. Some teachers may benefit by discussing this with their peers or by inviting a colleague in to observe a few classes.

The movement from conscious ineffectiveness to conscious effectiveness may take some time; it will take effort and commitment, and practice, failure, practice ... This is normal.

Management teams can facilitate such a process by running skills workshops, with a peer-support model as the outcome.

Changing skill repertoire

It takes time to change one's skill repertoire. The change involves not only the new skill (with its different verbal and non-verbal components), but also emotional change.

I used to argue with students — fine! It worked with those who weren't strong-willed, but with the students whose goal was clearly power, it never worked. When I started, some years back, to review and reassess my classroom discipline, I started to practise assertive dialogue in which one refuses to 'fight' on win/lose terms. In time the skill became almost second nature, but not before a phase (say, with argumentative students) in which I had consciously to apply what I'd planned to say and how I'd rehearsed it. During this phase, as I sought to say different things in arguments with students, I had ineffective as well as effective days (and still do), but I allowed myself a natural failure phase. I also *felt* uncomfortable doing something that didn't feel natural. That's OK. That's normal in skill development — but feelings (like attitudes) can be changed, especially by what we say to ourselves before, during

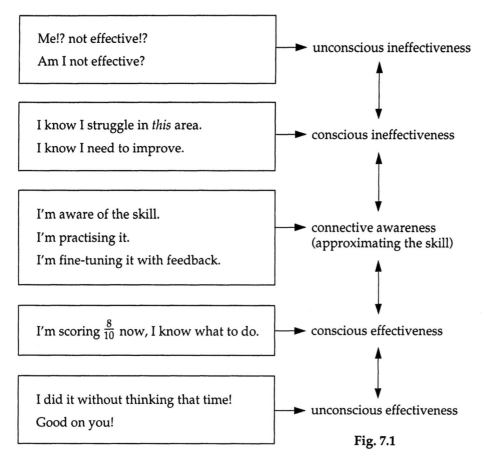

Me!? not effective!? Am I not effective?	→ unconscious ineffectiveness
I know I struggle in *this* area. I know I need to improve.	→ conscious ineffectiveness
I'm aware of the skill. I'm practising it. I'm fine-tuning it with feedback.	→ connective awareness (approximating the skill)
I'm scoring $\frac{8}{10}$ now, I know what to do.	→ conscious effectiveness
I did it without thinking that time! Good on you!	→ unconscious effectiveness

Fig. 7.1

and after stressful events. 'OK, it's clear that this new way doesn't feel right yet; it's also clear that it's a better way to deal with power-seeking students. Hang in there.'

However, during this process of skill development we're converting not only our verbal repertoire (what we say to or with argumentative and challenging students), but our old, involuntary emotional habits ('I'd like to maim him!'). The emotional arousal triggered by argumentative students is often a pull on our belief about power dominance in teacher–student transactions. This arousal is not merely automatic, we can learn to cognitively reassess such beliefs to see the student's goal for what it is and to avoid feeding it by using assertive dialogue. In this way we can train our emotional response towards a more voluntary state because we recognise where the arousal is coming from

and we have an action plan for dealing with the argumentative students (or colleagues). This reduces the *involuntary* competition from the older, (unconscious) emotional habits.

Nevertheless for a time there will be discomfort as you act out your new skills. Practising such things as tactical ignoring of, say, pouting, a student's sulky tone of voice, some calling-out attention seeking) may see you feeling frustrated. 'They shouldn't sulk like that!' Why? Perhaps we're saying that they *shouldn't* because of a belief that 'children should show respect to their teachers'. Disputing the 'demandingness' of that means looking at what we say to ourselves about such relational events. What is it about the behaviour that I say I can't stand? In what way do I get angry? He can't simply make me angry unless I believe something about how that relationship works ('he must be subordinate, in an ordinal position below me', 'he must show me respect').

I am responsible for what I choose to say to myself about events and relationships. I am also responsible for what I do. The management of behaviour involves thinking, emotion and doing. Initially there will be some cognitive dissonance between the old feelings associated by argumentative children and what you are choosing to believe and do (Festinger 1957). Any new skill, therefore, is not merely doing new things, it is believing and feeling (attitudinal) new things.

There will be ups and downs as you seek to apply new skills in stressful situations. But a skill is a bit like a habit. If a habit can be learned, it can be unlearned — given time and allowance for failure rate and personal forgiveness when you don't achieve the outcome you wanted.

To adapt Glickman (1991), 'Effective teachers are students of their own work-observing, contemplating adapting their behaviour and instruction as needs arise ...'.

Open doors, closed doors

As in all schools, there are members of staff who more readily accept a second pair of hands working in their rooms than others. Some staff members like the idea of another person helping out with process writing, taking a literature or maths group, working on the computer in the corner with a child or two, or whatever — just generally being part of a team of two people teaching together.

Then there are those who would rather keep the door closed or, if you are to help, would prefer that the group you are working with be withdrawn. That's OK, but you don't really want it to stay that way. The school's policy is towards team teaching and open doors. So how do you get around this? Tread softly, be patient and positive, and *be around*! Being the floating staff member, I try to get *them* used to me first. I pop in daily (probably drive them nuts at first!), make a point of talking to them, try to get to know them better in the staff room and corridors, take a real interest in them as people, engage them in discussion about children in their grades, look at and discuss their students' work with them (always focusing on the positives), involve them in team-planning sessions, keep offering help, continue taking the groups out but offering plenty of feedback and discussion about their progress, take their grades (for something they say they are not good at) while they are in the room, be ever watchful for the time when I can say: 'I'll help you with that. You'll need someone else to get through all that'.

It's possible to open the seemingly closed doors, but it's important to be prepared to be patient, positive, somewhat persuasive and pretty persistent! There can be real 'pay-offs' in getting to know the people behind the doors better. Most people really *do* have something special to offer to the life of the school, given the chance or the encouragement.

M.M.

Beginning teachers

Many first-year teachers come into schools unprepared for what they'll face, especially in schools serving a more non-compliant student population. Having worked with and tutored many first-year teachers, it is clear to me that fundamental skills of management and discipline have not been learned. It is reasonable to expect neophyte first-years to be inexperienced, but research has shown that these fundamental skills are often lacking:

- how to set up and enforce 'owned', fair, simple, workable classroom rules;
- how to set up basic procedures such as distribution, retrieval, marking of work;
- how to better organise a room for seating, work stations, co-operative group work;
- how to set up and use a discipline plan that includes positive corrective discipline (Rogers 1989, 1990);
- how to begin and end a lesson with minimum fuss;
- how to deal with argumentative students;
- how to manage a crisis situation — although this should be a whole-school approach anyway;
- how to follow up student behaviour after class, the ethics and practices of conferencing/counselling and developing behavioural contracts.

It is easy to feel overwhelmed as a beginning teacher: the newness of it all, the responsibility, so much to learn about this school, how to teach my subject (do you remember when?).

Notwithstanding the way we were often treated as first-years (shown the toilet, told 'Oh, read these — they might help' and 'You've got double maths with 9X on Friday afternoon — and oh, don't use any of those cups over there, use these — or better still bring your own — welcome to the school!'), it is important to recognise that any first-year teacher comes to your school *beginning* his or her career. Not only is it morally right to support that first year of professional life, it is practically sensible to create a support process.

1 Arrange a support group. If there are even two first-year teachers it is worth forming a group for them, perhaps with a second-year (or two). This group would meet as time permitted (preferably fortnightly) to support one another by allowing the opportunity to discuss needs, concerns and emerging problems. The first meeting prior to actual teaching needs to cover timetabling (first-years ought not to have the hardest class at all — that should go to the most competent), resources, how to crack the culture of this school, how to set up the first classes during the 'establishment phase' of the year (the rules, consequences, beginning and ending of lessons, a discipline plan) and how to get help with 'reputation' students.

Later meeting times need to be set aside to allow staff to talk about how they're progressing and to look for solutions to problems. This group needs a sensitive, committed teacher to lead it and, if possible, timetable allocation to indicate how important the school feels the issue to be.

2 If there is only one first-year teacher at the school, we can:
- check whether other schools in the cluster would be happy inviting your member of staff to join them;
- form a regional, after-school first-year group.

My colleagues and I have run many such after-school groups over six to ten sessions, using a common meeting place or rotating the meetings among schools. They included late afternoon tea, wine and snacks and two hours of discussion, a set topic (say, assertive skills in the classroom, how to get on with a recalcitrant principal [joke] or how to make behaviour contracts with students), and time to swap stories.

First-year teachers rate such groups as among the most significant professional assistance of their initial year (Rogers 1990). At a regional level they can be set up by educational psychologists, consultants and teachers from host schools.

Assessing staff interest

Some questions that would be asked of staff to ascertain awareness and interest in peer support are these.

- What levels of peer support exist currently in our school?
- How amenable are you to the concept of peer support (as treated in this discussion paper — or staff workshop, if there was one)?
- How amenable do you believe your colleagues are or would be to the concept of peer support?
- How could you (at classroom, faculty and management level) go about developing more effective peer support across the school? Do you have any suggestions? For example, what specific areas in the school particularly merit a peer-support approach? (See appendix VI.)
- Would you be willing to be involved in a peer-support group to explore more effective classroom management discipline?

Our peers are important. *Together* we make up the social fabric of our school. The OECD report (1989) makes the point that collaborative planning, shared decision making and collegial work in a framework of experimentation and evaluation is a clear characteristic of an effective school.

Admitting a concern or problem is the beginning of a solution...
~Teacher of 20 years experience

Conclusion

We live in a marginally sane world, a world where the human family has to live with the ambiguity of partial power, partial knowledge and partial freedom. This is life.

When we characteristically moan about life's problems and blame our feelings of anger, despair, loneliness or fear on others — when we demand daily, hourly that life should or shouldn't be this or that, that other's must do this or that — we do worse, we feel worse and those around us feel worse too.

As M. Scott-Peck (1990, p.13) has said:

> Life is difficult. This is a great truth, one of the greatest truths, because once we truly see this truth, we can transcend it ... They moan, more or less incessantly, noisily or subtly, about the enormity of their problems, their burdens and their difficulties as if life were generally easy, as if life should be easy. They voice their belief, noisily or subtly, that their difficulties represent a unique kind of affliction that should not be and that has somehow been especially visited upon them.
>
> Life is a series of problems. Do we want to moan about them or solve them?

Before we can effectively manage others, we need to effectively manage ourselves as best we can.

While others can encourage, direct and lead us, while others can show, teach and counsel us, we still have to manage ourselves — our time, our thinking, our emotions, our behaviour. While there are many 'techniques' and skills available to teachers in this area, you still have to deal with *you*. You have to live with *you*; you are the one feeling uptight, fed up, stressed out. You need to balance that fact with these skills and whatever support we can mobilise. Stressful emotion comes and goes — that's life, but where it is a regular part of life it may be that the beliefs that underlie those feelings need challenging and reshaping so that further stress is minimised and does not significantly interfere with our goals.

- Be aware that emotion and self-talk are powerfully related.
- When you're feeling really low, frustrated, stressed out, tune in to what you are saying. What's the basis of it?
  What am I saying to myself here?
  What do I characteristically say about such events?
- Practice 'disputing' negative, inaccurate, demanding thinking. Replace it with accurate, reasonable, realistic, confidence-provoking 'talk' — both self-talk and 'public talk'.
- Look at the events and situations and people that seem to create stress in you. What can reasonably be done? Ask others to help. Ask yourself: 'What support can I utilise in and out of school to enable myself to live and work less stressfully?' Create a simple plan to make it work for you.

We all have difficulty in thinking rationally. After all, the world often appears as gristle, grit, work and pain. Be vigorous and regular in questioning your dysfunctional beliefs and self-talk and work on productive, useful beliefs — and the odds are that you'll not get as upset as often or for as long.

This book is about managing stress. William Glasser (1991) has made the point that effective teaching is one of the most difficult and demanding professions. Daily we interact with students whose needs go well beyond the lessons and educational aims of the school in which we teach. We, too, bring our 'emotional baggage' into the relational life of a school.

The emotional climate inherent in the demands of our role means that stress is both inevitable and natural. The degree to which it interferes with our coping resources, however, will depend on how well we can balance these demands with those resources.

One of the more encouraging trends in schools today is the move towards whole-school policy and practice, and a commitment to peer support. In his book *Awakenings* the psychiatrist Oliver Sacks says that 'we cannot really separate individual events from social events' (p. 268). Our lives impact on, and affect, one another.

I believe it is possible (as experience and research show) to gain in a school a balance between individual accountability and peer support — a climate in which teachers believe and can feel comfortable in sharing their needs, concerns and problems and in which a commitment to professional development, based on peer support, will find the solutions our schools need to fulfil their professional and social obligations.

It is my hope that this book will contribute to this process. Best wishes.

BILL ROGERS
Melbourne, September 1991

Staff survey:
Classroom discipline and management

This survey would be conducted across the school and time set aside for discussion of responses. The discipline welfare committee would use the results to plan workshops and policy development.

Classroom discipline (major survey)

1 What sort of disruptions occur in your classroom at present?
   - Can you rank them in terms of most to least pressing (i.e. frustrating to your right to teach and students right to learn)?
   - Can you note how regular (frequent) such behaviours are?
   (Please be specific — it will help.)

2 In what subject areas do you notice these behaviours occurring?
   At what time of day?
   On which days of the week?

3 What year level seems to be most pressing? Do any particular students stand out? Please give name(s).

4 What strategies do you presently employ in managing disruptive behaviours? What approaches do you consider most effective? Why?

5 Classroom rules.
   (a) What are they, specifically?
   (b) How were they communicated to the students?
   (c) What consequences do you have in place to apply when they are significantly infringed?

6 Exit of students (directing students from the room for seriously disruptive behaviour).
   (a) What *sort of behaviours* do you exit students from the room for?
   (b) How often?
      - once a session?
      - once a week?
      - once or twice a term?
      - less often?
   (c) In what *subject areas* does this usually occur?
   (d) Who do you refer exited students to? (When you send them out, who and where do they go to?)
   (e) How do the students go? Supported by a note? On your direction? With another student? Using other systems?
   (f) If the student refuses to leave, what do you do? What is your 'plan B'?
   (g) What follow-up do you specifically do with any student you exit?
   (h) On what basis do you (i) effect some conflict resolution, (ii) enable the student to renegotiate entry back to your classroom or subject area?
   (i) Do you have any concerns about the school's exit and follow-up policy as it is presently practised? What are they?

7 What areas of school policy regarding classroom/school discipline do you believe are working well?

What areas do you note that concern you?

What suggestions can you note for improvement?

Classroom management

8 Are there any areas of management that you need assistance with (e.g. time/workload; marking processes; mixed-ability teaching; room organisation of seating, work stations, group work)?

Thank you for your co-operation. The results of this survey will be communicated to you as part of the school commitment to a whole-school approach to discipline and welfare.

Questions on exit/time-out policy

1 Have we surveyed the staff on this issue? If so, what did we discover about the following concerns: frequency, particular areas, particular students, apparent patterns, sort of time-out being used (sitting outside class, being sent to colleagues, other)?

2 What is our present policy? Is it owned by staff? Is it published? Is there a clear purpose for use of time-out? Does it vary for year and faculty levels? Why?

3 Where do we expect teachers to send overly disruptive, aggressive, safety-threatening students?

4 What happens if a student is unwilling to leave?

5 What follow-up provisions are expected?

6 What role do we expect of the initiating teacher, the parent and the support staff?

7 How do we distinguish exit/time-out from counselling and conferencing/contracting provisions?

For the individual teacher

8 What are you characteristically using time-out provisions for? (If it is more a control measure than a legitimate consequence, you may need to reconsider your short-term corrective discipline plan.)

9 How do you follow up the classroom incident that necessitated exit and time-out provisions?

10 What longer term support do you need to follow up the exit student?

11 Whom can you rely on for support in using exit/time-out measures if there is no clear school policy?

12 How will you go about setting up a supportive time-out policy as an individual classroom/subject teacher?

Out-of-classroom discipline plan

Review process

The out-of-classroom discipline plan has been developed to give students, teachers and parents a clear understanding of the school's expectations of behaviour outside the classroom.

There is an expectation that teachers, whether on yard duty or not, will deal with misbehaviour in a consistent manner, as outlined in the grid following. Consistent misbehaviour will lead to school-wide supportive action being taken.

This plan should be implemented, evaluated and refined in the following manner:

1 Within the first two weeks of each school year, the principal and teachers will remind students of the rules and consequences of the school-wide discipline plan.

2 In discussing the classroom discipline plan, teachers will also review the out-of-classroom plan. The time spent on this will depend on the familiarity of students with the plan; for example, younger students and those newer to the school will need more time than older students.

3 In particular, Prep students should be involved in an intensive program that outlines safety in the playground, use of the equipment, ways of playing games, etc. Special attention will be given to this matter by Prep teachers.

4 Within the first month of each year, the school discipline plans will be reviewed at a staff meeting.

5 The Student Council should participate in an annual evaluation and refinement of this plan during term 3 of every year or as an urgent need arises. It is an expectation that student representatives will involve their classes in this evaluation. Any refinements arising from this evaluation must be discussed and agreed to by staff.

Out-of-classroom discipline grid

Rule about	Area covered	Example	Consequences
Movement	Within the building (e.g. corridors) Late arrival to Assembly In the playground	We will remember to stay in our designated play areas and be punctual at all times. Walk quietly, don't run.	While the following strategies are presented hierarchically, they could be used in any sequence. • Rule reminder • Verbal apology • Written apology • Isolation from peers – accompanying yard-duty teacher – to an area/zone in the playground to 'cool off'
Communication	Assemblies Movement between rooms Lining up outside rooms	At Assembly or when moving to specialist lessons or going into school, we will move quietly so that we can hear what is being said and will not disturb others.	• Withdrawal from playground – to administrative personnel – to a specific time-out area Use to be determined at the beginning of each year
Treatment	The way we treat one another (no sexism, no put-downs) Manners	In the playground, all people are to be treated fairly. This means that we don't put people down because they look different from us, have different backgrounds or come from different countries.	• Loss of privileges – no use of equipment – missing excursions – withdrawal to specific areas
Safety	Use of playground equipment Dangerous toys, rough games/play, stone-throwing Movement around blind corners Banned items, e.g. glass bottles, cans, chewing gum	At school, we will be careful when using all equipment and will look after ourselves and others.	• Any student sent to vice-principal's or principal's office or time-out area will have his or her name recorded • Refer to School-wide Supportive Action
Problem solving	The way we fix up problems among one another	At our school, if we have a problem with another student we will try to talk it over quietly. If we can't solve it, we'll ask the teacher on duty for help. We will try to settle our problems without fighting. We will try to be responsible for our own behaviour and punctuality.	
Learning	Outdoor activities Behaviour on camps and excursions	We will respect the opinions of others when involved in outdoor activities.	

Developing a playground behaviour-management policy

Playground supervision is not the most pleasant of our duties as teachers. Daily we face students who argue and fight, who play in out-of-bounds areas, who come and tell us that 'so and so has done this or that' (and, of course, they may well be telling the truth), who drop litter, who play in unsafe ways and who tease, spit, swear ...

If our supervision is going to be more effective in the sense that it minimises unnecessary confrontation yet encourages and challenges ownership of and responsibility for behaviour by the student, then a whole-school focus is necessary. Students are adept at playing one teacher off against another, and widely different approaches by teachers or inconsistent enforcement of rules and consequences only sends mixed messages.

A playground behaviour-management policy requires that staff (and students, where appropriate):

1 clarify what is currently occurring in playground behaviour (frequency and degree of disruptive behaviour);
2 examine usefulness of current rules, consequences;
3 decide what to do in both the short term (on the spot) and the long term with typical disruptive behaviours such as fighting, teasing or swearing;
4 develop a management plan for staff that will establish a rational and consistent approach to playground supervision and management.

Staff survey

It will be helpful for staff to think about the following questions prior to a planning meeting. The questions will enable them to clarify the current situation before developing policy directions.

1 What are the current playground disruptions you regularly deal with when on yard duty? List them in terms of *how frequently* you observe them. What actually happens, as you see it?

2 Can you rank disruptions in terms of seriousness and frequency? For example, we all have to deal with fighting on yard duty, but it can be helpful to distinguish between play fighting (in varying degrees), serious fighting, in which hostile and aggressive intent (and serious outcome) is involved, and bullying.

3 Do the disruptions occur in any particular age group?

4 Do they occur in any particular area of the playground?

5 Is morning play generally worse than lunch or afternoon, or vice versa?

6 What rules currently exist relevant to playground behaviour?
   • Can you list them?
   • How specific are they? Do they address the actual behaviour?
   • Do you believe there are too many, too few, or even certain unnecessary rules?
   • What changes do you believe may be necessary?

7 Can you note what you characteristically say and do when you deal with the following occurrences?
   • fighting (play fighting/aggressive fighting);

- swearing, spitting and put-downs;
- teasing, tale-telling (distinguish legitimate reporting);
- litter (general), and litter clearly seen dropped;
- out-of-bounds areas (no-ball, no-go areas);
- unsafe play;
- smoking.

8 What consequences currently exist for serious breaches of playground rules? Is there a time-out policy for students in the playground?

9 Are there any other issues you wish to raise?

Staff discussion on policy review

The answers to these questions will enable staff to clarify the nature, extent and seriousness of disruptive behaviour in the playground.

The discussion around the questions will enable a consensus to be reached on how best to develop a management plan. As staff discuss the answers to the questions, they can determine what direction the policy ought to take. The process of discussion and 'ownership' is essential for a more coherent and consistent approach to management and supervision on non-classroom behaviour.

Through this process, we ought to be able to clarify the rules and develop a strategy plan that can address both management issues (number and quality of seating, quality of shade areas, play facilities, litter bins) and discipline issues (from how we deal with teasing through to the non-negotiables, such as aggression, threats to safety or violence).

An action plan for discipline ought to outline how we can best deal with the disruptive behaviours we commonly face. By sharing effective strategies, even discussing better things to say when we're under pressure, our management and discipline will become more accurately targeted and more consistent.

When reviewing policy, it will be necessary to determine how clear, fair and enforceable our rules are. Are they expressed in terms that address the behaviour? Or are they merely a list of 'don'ts'?

Rules are there, after all, to protect the rights of all members of the school community and to invoke their responsibility.

A policy will not be written overnight. It may take a few meetings to draft what we want to do and to trial our management plan. A timeline for trial, review and evaluation will enable us to fine-tune as needs arise.

Student involvement

It is also useful to involve students in the survey process and to give them feedback as the policy develops.

Grade teachers can discuss playground behaviour with their classes..

- What is going on in the playground?
- Is there anything that causes you concern?

Where students note particular behaviours, ask how frequent and how serious they are. Get them to clarify their views.

Ask them what they think teachers ought to do. 'What do you see teachers doing when they observe fighting or swearing or teasing? What do you think teachers ought to do then? Why?'

Teachers may want to discuss consequences with students, too (it will be helpful to distinguish between punishment and logical, reasonable consequences).

The information gathered from students can augment the staff survey.

Playground questionnaire

This questionnaire could be adapted for use by class groups, staff groups and the school council.

1 What are the areas of our school playground that need improvement?
   (a) Is seating adequate? Is more needed? Does it need fixing? Where is it? Is it painted? Are there any outside lunch tables?
   (b) Trees and potted shrubs or plants add beauty. Are there any areas that could benefit from greenery? Ask your class or home group.
   (c) Are there enough shade areas? Are there any 'hot spots' that could benefit from a shade-over (a frame with shade cloth filtering light)?
   (d) Are the covered areas adequate for rainy days?
   (e) Are there appropriate guide rails for canteen queues? Are canteen times monitored in large schools? Are support staff involved in management-training programs?

2 Play equipment.
   (a) Do you have any comments about the safety of our play equipment? Are students using it adequately protected by the presence of bark-clippings on the ground?
   (b) Are we aware of where playground accidents occur? Does where they occur have any connection with the state of equipment?
   (c) Are children allowed to borrow adequate play equipment from the phys.ed. department? Do you have equipment in each classroom (at primary level) — skipping-ropes, bats, balls, hoops, etc.
   (d) What about wet-day duty and play equipment? What are we currently doing? How are staff rostered? Are *all* staff rostered (including senior staff)?

3 What about use of library or art rooms as an adjunct to the playground? The rooms could be opened as an alternative means of recess use (students would have this as a rostered option).

4 When Preps first start, can we roster a 'buddy-system' for a term to settle them into the social life of the playground?

Professional relationships in peer support — questionnaire

1 In what ways do others provide you with a sense of security and 'safety' here?

2 What common network of interests and concerns do you have with fellow teachers?

3 In what way are your skills, abilities, contribution and worth acknowledged?

4 What guidance and professional advice do you receive? From whom? Do you trust and account as authoritative and trustworthy the persons and advice you receive?

5 Are there people here that you can count on for assistance in any circumstance?

6 Are you in a position, here, where you have an opportunity to nurture another? To provide for the wellbeing of another? In what ways?

7 In what ways would you want realistic support from:
   (a) your colleagues?
   (b) your year-level co-ordinator (or head of department)?
   (c) your principal or deputy principal?

8 In what ways can we develop a 'culture of support' in our school?

The flow chart on the following page illustrates a process devised to highlight the benefits of peer support.

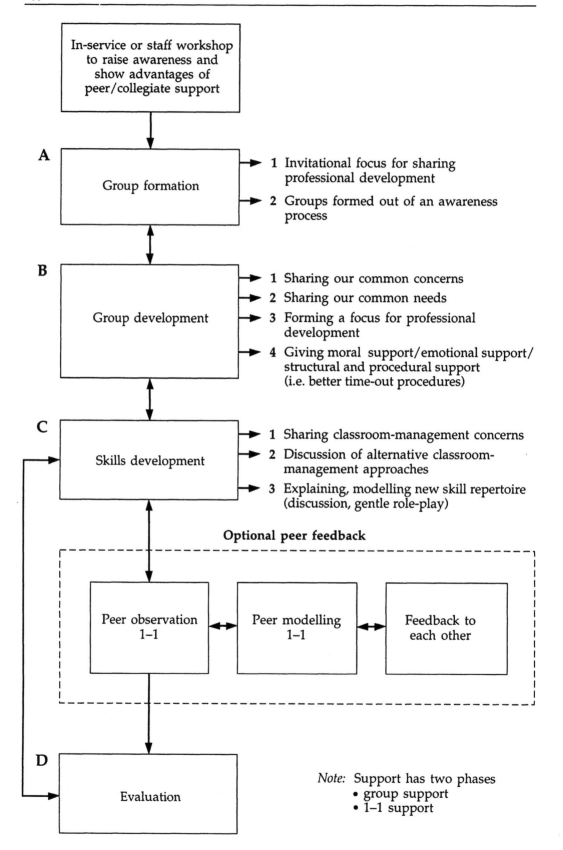

In-service or staff workshop to raise awareness and show advantages of peer/collegiate support

A Group formation

1 Invitational focus for sharing professional development

2 Groups formed out of an awareness process

B Group development

1 Sharing our common concerns
2 Sharing our common needs
3 Forming a focus for professional development
4 Giving moral support/emotional support/ structural and procedural support (i.e. better time-out procedures)

C Skills development

1 Sharing classroom-management concerns
2 Discussion of alternative classroom-management approaches
3 Explaining, modelling new skill repertoire (discussion, gentle role-play)

Optional peer feedback

Peer observation 1–1 ↔ Peer modelling 1–1 ↔ Feedback to each other

D Evaluation

Note: Support has two phases
• group support
• 1–1 support

Bibliography

Adler, V. 1989,'Little control = lots of stress', *Psychology Today*, April, pp. 18–19.

Baars, C.W. 1979, *Feeling and Healing Your Emotions*, Logos International, New York.

Bernard, M. 1990, *Taking the Stress out of Teaching*, Collins Dove, Melbourne.

Bernard, M.E. & Joyce, M.R. 1985, *Rational Emotive Therapy with Children and Adolescents: Theory, Treatment, Strategies, Preventative Methods*, J. Wiley & Sons, New York.

Braiker, H.B. 1989, 'The power of self-talk', *Psychology Today*, December, pp. 23–7.

Brandes, D. & Ginnis, P. 1986, *A Guide to Student-centred Learning*, Basil Blackwell, Oxford.

Buckman, R. 1987, in *Punch*, 11 February, p. 26.

Burns, D. D. 1989, *The Good Feeling Handbook*, in Braiker, op. cit.

The Carnegie Foundation for the Advancement of Teaching 1990, *The Conditions of Teaching: A State-by-State Analysis*, Princeton University Press, Princeton, New Jersey.

Charles, C.M. 1985, *Building Classroom Discipline: From Models to Practice*, 2nd edn, Longman, New York.

Colarelli, S. 1989, in *Psychology Today*, March, p. 44.

Coopersmith, S. 1967, *The Antecedents of Self-esteem*, Freeman, San Francisco.

Cowin, M. et al. 1985, *Positive School Discipline: A Guide to Developing Policy*, Parents and Friends of Monnington, Melbourne.

De Bono, E. 1986, *Conflicts: A Better Way to Resolve Them*, Penguin, Harmondsworth.

Dreikurs, R. 1968, *Psychology in the Classroom: A Manual for Teachers*, 2nd edn, Harper & Row, New York.

—— 1971, *Social Equality: The Challenge of Today*, Contemporary Books Inc., Chicago.

Dreikurs, R., Grunwald, B. & Pepper, F. 1982, *Maintaining Sanity in the Classroom*, 2nd edn, Harper & Row, New York.

Edwards, C. 1977, 'RET in high school', *Rational Living*, 12, pp. 10–12.

Ellis, A. & Harper, R. 1975, *A New Guide to Rational Living*, Wilshire Book Co., North Hollywood, California.

Elton Report 1989, *Discipline in Schools, Report of the Committee of Inquiry*, Her Majesty's Stationery Office, London.

Festinger, L. 1957, *A Theory of Cognitive Dissonance*, Stanford University Press, Stanford, California.

Frankl, V.E. 1963, *Man's Search for Meaning*, Simon & Schuster/Gulf & Western, New York.

Glasser, W. 1986, *Control Theory in the Classroom*, Harper & Row, New York.

—— 1991, *The Quality School: Managing Students Without Coercion*, Harper & Row, New York.

Glenn, H.S. & Nelsen, J. 1987, *Raising Self-Reliant Children in a Self-Indulgent World*, Prima Publishing, Rocklin, California.

Glickman, C. 1991, 'Pretending not to know what we know', *Educational Leadership*, May, pp. 4–9.

Guskey, T.R. 1986, 'Staff development and the process of teacher change', *Educational Researcher*, vol. 15 (5), May.

Hamilton, P. 1986, Study noted in Szaday, C. 1989, *Addressing Behaviour Problems in Australian Schools*, ACER, Hawthorn, Victoria.

Hauk, P.A. 1967, *The Rational Management of Children*, Libra Publishers, New York.

—— 1977, 'Irrational parenting styles', Ellis, A. & Greiger, R. (eds), *Handbook of Rational-Emotive Therapy*, Institute for Rational Living, New York.

Horney, K. 1945, *Our Inner Conflict*, Norton, New York.

Hosking, S. 1985, 'Stress: an organisational perspective', *VTU Journal*, vol. 11, no. 3.

Jarvis, W. 1975, *Discover Yourself and Live*, Nelson, London.

Johnson, D.W. & Johnson, B.T. 1989, *Leading the Cooperative School*, Interaction Book Co., Minnesota.

Jones, P. & Tucker, E. (eds) 1990, *Mixed Ability Teaching—Classroom Experiences in English, ESL, Mathematics and Science*, St Clair Press, Rozelle, NSW.

Kounin, J. 1971, *Discipline and Group Management in Classrooms*, Holt, Rhinehart & Winston, New York.

Kyriacou, C. 1981, 'Social support and occupational stress among school teachers', *Educational Studies*, vol. 7, pp. 55–60.

—— 1986, *Effective Teaching in Schools*, Basil Blackwell, Oxford.

—— 1987, 'Teacher stress and burnout: an international review', *Educational Research*, vol. 29, no. 2, June, pp. 146–52.

Lancaster, R. 1985, *Stress*, Video Arts Ltd, London.

Lazarus, R.S. & Folkman, S. 1984, *Stress: Appraisal and Coping*, Springer, New York.

Lowe, J. & Istance, D. 1989, *Schools and Quality* (an international report), OECD, Paris.

Macleod, R. 1987, *Strategies for Tackling Teacher Stress*, Teachers Federation of Victoria, Richmond, Vic.

Maultsby, M.C. 1977, 'Basic principles of intensive rational behaviour therapy: theories, goals, techniques and advantages', Wolfe, J.L. & Brands, E. (eds), *Twenty Years of Rational Therapy*, Institute for Rational Living, New York.

Miller, L. 1989, 'To beat stress, don't relax: get tough', *Psychology Today*, December, pp. 62–3.

Montgomery, B. 1986, *Coping with Stress*, Pitman Health Information Series, Melbourne.

Montgomery, B. & Evans, L. 1984, *You and Stress: A Guide to Successful Living*, Thomas Nelson, Melbourne.

Morgan, D.P. & Jenson, W.R. 1988, *Teaching Behaviourally Disordered Students: Preferred Practices*, Merrill Publishing Co., Toronto.

Myklehun, Reidar J. 1984, 'Teacher stress: perceived and objective sources and quality of life', *Scandinavian Journal of Education Research*, vol. 28(1), March, pp. 17–45.

Nelsen, J. 1981, *Positive Discipline*, Ballantyne Books, New York.

Noble, G. & Watkins, M. 1988, 'Teachers' work: morale in public education', *Education Australia*, issue 2.

Otto, R. 1985, *Teachers under Stress*, Hill of Content, Melbourne.

Pratt, J. 1978, 'Perceived stress among teachers', *Educational Review*, 30, pp. 3–14.

Parkes, K.R. 1986, 'Coping in stressful episodes: the role of individual differences, environmental factors, and situational characteristics', *Journal of Personality and Social Psychology*, vol. 51, no. 6, pp. 1277–99.

Positive Discipline: Improving Behaviour in the Classroom 1990, Department of Education & the Arts, Hobart, Tasmania.

Richardson, S. & Izard, J. 1990, *Practical Approaches to Resolving Behaviour Problems*, ACER, Hawthorn, Victoria.

Robertson, J. 1989, *Effective Classroom Control: Understanding Teacher-Pupil Relationships*, 2nd edn, Hodder & Stoughton, London.

Rogers, W. 1989a, *Decisive Discipline: Every Move You Make, Every Step You Take*, Institute of Educational Administration, Geelong, Victoria (video-learning package).

—— 1989b, *Making a Discipline Plan*, Thomas Nelson, Melbourne.

—— 1990, *You Know the Fair Rule*, ACER, Hawthorn, Victoria.

—— 1991a, *Dealing with Procrastination*, set no. 1, ACER, Hawthorn, Victoria.

—— 1991b, 'Attention deficit disorder', *Behaviour Problems Bulletin*, vol. 5, no. 1, May, pp. 12–19.

Russell, D.W., Altmaier, E. & Van Velzen, D. 1987, 'Job-related stress: social support and burnout among classroom teachers', *Journal of Applied Psychology*, May, vol. 72, no. 2, pp. 269–74.

Rutter, M. et al. 1979, *Fifteen Thousand Hours: Secondary Schools and their Effects on Children*, Open Books, London.

Safran, S.P., Safran, J.S. & Barcikowski, R.S. 1985, 'Differences in teacher tolerance: an illusory phenomenon?', *Behaviour Disorders*, pp. 11–15.

Scott Peck, M. 1990, *The Road Less Travelled*, Arrow Books, London.

Selye, H. 1975, *Stress without Distress*, Signet, New York.

—— 1978, *The Stress of Life*, McGraw-Hill, New York.

Slee, R. (ed.) 1988, *Discipline and Schools: A Curriculum Perspective*, Macmillan, Melbourne.

Smith, M. 1981, *When I Say No I Feel Guilty*, Bantam Books, Toronto.

Smith, P.K. & Thompson, D. 1991, *Practical Approaches to Bullying*, David Fulton, London.

Tavris, C. 1982, 'Anger defused', *Psychology Today*, November.

Teacher Stress in Victoria: A Survey of Teachers' Views 1989, Applied Psychology Research Group, Ministry of Education, Melbourne.

Trotter, R.J. 1987, 'Stop blaming yourself (the research of Robert Seligman), *Psychology Today*, February, pp. 31–9.

Wilson, B.L. & Corcoran, T.B. 1988, *Successful Secondary Schools: Visions of Excellence in American Public Education*, Falmer Press, London.

Woodhouse, D.A., Hall, E. & Wooster, A.D. 1985, 'Taking control of stress in teaching', *British Journal of Educational Psychology*, 55, pp. 119–23.

Wragg, J. 1989, *Talk Sense to Yourself: A Program for Children and Adolescents*, ACER, Hawthorn, Victoria.

▼
About the author

William A. Rogers is a educational consultant currently working independently. A teacher by profession, Rogers has also been a consultant to the Ministry of Education in Victoria and to the Elton Report, *Discipline in Schools* (1989). He has lectured widely in Australia and the United Kingdom, taking seminars, in-services and lecture programs, and has developed peer-support programs for teachers (over 60 000 in the last six years). He works in all levels of education (primary, post-primary and tertiary) running in-service programs for teachers, lecturing widely at universities and working with parent groups and students.

Rogers is the author of a number of articles, books and other publications concerning these issues.